Praise for
Relationship ReFresh

"This book is full of deep personal life situations that Thomas uses as a simple guide to growing your intimate relationships. It is easy to read, and the principles are easy to apply. Thomas ends the book with this question, 'How will you make the experience and expression of love your life's pursuit?' I say, within the cover of this book are all the tools you would need for deep and long-lasting love. *Relationship ReFresh* is a must-read for the lover within all of us!"

—**Georgiana Kovell,** author of *Women on a Mission*, founder of Millions of Women Strong

"If you are looking for an owner's manual for building your intimate relationships, this is it. Too often, we feel like we are not in the driver's seat. *Relationship ReFresh* will not only put you in the driver's seat, but will become your owner's manual. A lifetime guarantee for a relationship filled with satisfaction and fulfillment is packed within this book."

—**Jen Coken,** author of *When I Die, Take My Panties*; speaker, author, and international executive coach

"*Relationship ReFresh* is an excellent collection of tools for managing and growing relationships. I love how practical the work is and how easy he makes it to apply. The way Thomas connects with his reader by using authentic self-experiences makes its application very real. I am still shaking from the fear of his story when he discovered being left all alone in the middle of the ocean. Thomas is a master of the body of distinctions of love."

—**Ralph White,** best-selling author of *12 Steps to Success in Business Life*, CEO, business coach, Possibilities Unlimited, Inc.

"This book is easy to read. It showed me my blind spots and was very eye-opening. I realized the bad behaviors that I still have in relationships and how to shift these behaviors so my partner feels loved, seen, and known. I am very grateful for this book because now I feel like I am more capable to have a healthy long-term relationship. The numerous examples in the book also helped me see that I am not alone. Thank you Thomas, for writing this extraordinary book."

—**Suzanne Mueller-Heinz,** author of *Loveable: 21 Practices for Being in a Loving & Fulfilling Relationship*, international dating and love life coach and speaker; CEO of Loveablize

"I have known Thomas for many years and always seen him as a person who lives and speaks from his heart. His new book is a precious example of how a person who lives from their heart can make a huge difference in the lives of others. Thomas is an expert in supporting people in going beyond their self-sabotaging and habitual patterns to not only live happier lives but to experience deep intimacy in relationships. If you're looking for peace in your lives and relationships, this book is a wonderful blueprint for attainment."

—**Michael Stone,** author, teacher, and radio host

Relationship
REFRESH

Relationship
REFRESH

Achieve Your Deepest Desire
and Experience True, Lasting Love!

Thomas Kuster

RIVER GROVE
BOOKS

This publication is designed to provide accurate and authoritative information in regard to the subject matter covered. It is sold with the understanding that the publisher and author are not engaged in rendering legal, accounting, or other professional services. Nothing herein shall create an attorney-client relationship, and nothing herein shall constitute legal advice or a solicitation to offer legal advice. If legal advice or other expert assistance is required, the services of a competent professional should be sought.

Published by River Grove Books
Austin, TX
www.rivergrovebooks.com

Copyright © 2021 Thomas Kuster

All rights reserved.

Thank you for purchasing an authorized edition of this book and for complying with copyright law. No part of this book may be reproduced, stored in a retrieval system, or transmitted by any means, electronic, mechanical, photocopying, recording, or otherwise, without written permission from the copyright holder.

Distributed by River Grove Books

Design and composition by Greenleaf Book Group
Cover design by Greenleaf Book Group

Publisher's Cataloging-in-Publication data is available.

Print ISBN: 978-1-63299-431-8

eBook ISBN: 978-1-63299-432-5

First Edition

*For my spouse, Rafael, our relationship
and every relationship that is
ultimately influenced by our work.*

Contents

Prologue   xiii
    Looking Back
    How to Use This Book

1: Laying the Foundation for Love Sparks   1
    Habits and the Brain
    Habits Identified
    Understanding the Elements
    The Deconstruction Model
    The Do-Over Game

2: Your Deepest Desire (Love Spark #1)   19
    Listen to Your Heart
    How Do You Satisfy Your Deepest Desire?
    Giving Away Your Deepest Desire

3: Why? (Love Spark #2)   29
    Asking the Question
    Cocktails Anyone?
    Conditions of Satisfaction
    Rise to the Top
    A Couple's Why

4: Letting Go of Judgment (Love Spark #3)   41
    Being Together
    Is This True Love?
    Easier Said than Done
    Connection through Acceptance

5: Stop! Look! Listen! (Love Spark #4)   49
    Heart*aches* and Heart*breaks*
    Tender Spots versus Emotional Wounds
    Don't Resist the Pain
    Getting to the Love Spark
    Stop! Look! Listen!

6: Full Moments, on Purpose (Love Spark #5)   61
    Full Moments
    Now for Yours
    The Art of Design
    Three Elements

7: For-Giveness (Love Spark #6)   71
    Developing the Language of Love
    Apologizing: The Plan
    Here's How

8: Sliding Door Moments (Love Spark #7)   79
    Opening and Closing
    The Pathway to Trust
    The Two of You
    The Truth
    When Your Partner Breaks Your Trust
    Take Advantage of Sliding Door Moments

9: The Couple's Code of Honor   91
    "Shoulds"
    "Musts"
    Raising Your Standards
    Couple's Code of Honor
    Our Couple's Code of Honor

10: Rules of Engagement   101
    Avoiding Landmines
    Can You Remain Close?
    Rules of Engagement
    Finding Common Ground
    Make Repair Attempts as You Go

Contents

11: The Friction That Binds Us — 113
   Generating Fire
   The Magic Bullet
   A Necessary Ingredient
   Ebb and Flow

12: Keeping Intimacy Alive — 119
   It's an Attitude
   Could There Possibly Be Anything More?

13: Relationship ReFresh — 127
   How Do You ReFresh?
   The Daily Grind
   Right and Wrong
   How to Get Your Love Experience

Epilogue — 135

Acknowledgments — 137

About the Author — 139

Prologue

It's 1963 and pouring rain outside. I'm sitting in the front room of our little rental house, watching the droplets fall and splash into a puddle on the other side of the window.

It's hard to say how long I've been sitting here; it seems like hours. I'm a thinker, a kid who spends a great deal of time in his head. And as I watch the rain, I feel peaceful inside.

The rain drowns out my mom and dad arguing in their bedroom. I don't know how often they do this, but I think it's very often, and even as a kid, I know this isn't good. I'm sad, but thankful for the rain.

I wonder how I can help Mom and Dad be peaceful, too? What can I be when I grow up to solve the problems that they cannot?

This five-year-old kid thinks too much.

Looking Back

As far back as I can remember, a peaceful environment was important to me. With all the chaos at home, I thought it was my job to be the peacemaker. The funny thing is, you can only be a peacemaker where there is no peace.

Mom was barely eighteen years old when I was born, and my

Dad was not quite twenty. They had a hard time getting along with one another. I never understood it at the time because I was just a kid, but now I realize they were kids, too.

I can't imagine how it must have been for them. Yet even if the environment was emotionally unhealthy, my brothers and I knew we were loved.

I also know now, as an adult, how fortunate I was to have them as parents, though hearing them fight was traumatic. Trauma relates to an experience that is unbearable, and for this kid, my parents' fighting was unbearable.

I was a quiet and relatively passive child, thoughtful and loving. When peace was disrupted around me, it felt as though my body was crashing in on itself. I gave up the right to be happy until Mom and Dad could be happy.

My brothers and I grew up with the Catholic faith. The church was my first exposure to peace. By the time I was seven years old, I had decided to become a priest. I thought that was the answer.

"If I become a priest and a teacher," I thought, "then I could learn how to bring peace to Mom and Dad, and then they could be happy."

I tried hard to make my parents' relationship better because I wanted stability for our family. In the end, I didn't become a priest but rather a student of life and a lifetime learner.

Mom and Dad were together for fifty years until my Dad died. As the years went by, they became more committed to peace, too, and I saw some happiness between them. I never gave up, and they were genuinely open to my ideas and input.

Over the years, I have pursued and practiced many different methods of bringing peace to myself and others. In the early 1980s, I trained in the work of Zig Ziglar, a well-known motivational speaker at the time. Zig gave me a foundation and a hunger for learning about people and going beneath their exteriors. Tony Robbins and his book *Unlimited Power* reignited the principles I learned from Zig and gave me some direction.

Sales was my game. I managed, trained, and developed groups in engagement selling. But I didn't see my future until I was introduced to personal transformation techniques, starting with *Love Is Letting Go of Fear* by Dr. Gerald Jampolsky and doing the self-study program "A Course In Miracles" more times than I can count.

I wrote a number of training programs until 1995, when I founded the principles that I have now spent decades establishing: "Partners for Life."

The next seventeen years I spent leading transformational programs for the world's largest self-development company. Being a thought leader, a student, and a trainer was fulfilling for me at the deepest levels. Nothing prepared me more for what life had in store. I trained, developed, and coached well over ten thousand people, and then "The Stages of Love," my California-based coaching practice, was born.

As an Emotional Health Practitioner and Couples Coach, I've applied everything I've learned to my coaching practice and to the writing of this book.

How to Use This Book

This book includes some simple yet essential workbook activities that will serve you well on your journey to having a successful and happy partnership. I also suggest reading Chapters One through Three in one sitting, if you are able.

To get the most out of each exercise, stop and complete each one as you go. None of the activities are overly challenging. They require only honesty about your feelings and thoughts at the moment.

You'll uncover what I call your Bad Relationship Habit(s), and your Deepest Desire. You will also reveal the reasons why being in a relationship is so essential for you, which I refer to as your Why. When you find these for yourself, the satisfaction you get from *all* your relationships will increase dramatically.

My memory of growing up amid constant chaos is no longer seen through a child's eyes. I see it now for what it was: a childhood with kids for parents. They were not equipped to raise children, and how could they be? Their parents were hardly equipped themselves. Because they were babies of the Great Depression, survival naturally became their priority. They paid very little attention to happiness and peace of mind.

I believe that all people deserve peace of mind and that it is naturally available for everyone. I also think that kids deserve to be happy, to have happy homes, and to have happy parents.

I wrote this book for ALL the kids in the world—the little ones growing up and the big ones who never got the chance to really be happy.

I also wrote this book for me. Not the writer-me, but the husband-me who needs to keep my relationship as exciting and fulfilling as possible.

My spouse Rafael and I met more than twenty years ago, and we married in 2015. It wasn't a huge priority for us until the legal battles for same sex marriage were settled. He has been a barber for close to fifty years and is now semi-retired. All the stories about the two of us in this book are true, and I am grateful he is a such a good sport, letting me share them with you.

I hope you get as much out of reading this book as I have writing it. It will help you develop Good Relationship Habits. I call them "Love Sparks."

Couples who use Love Sparks in their relationships will eliminate barriers to their ability to express and experience love at any moment. *Any* moment!

They will achieve peace of mind and provide happy homes for their kids.

Yes! You can have a supercharged relationship!

You *can* have your relationships work!

You *can* have a life filled with satisfaction, peace, and happiness!

Using Love Sparks will evoke higher levels of trust. You and your partner will feel more peace and attain more happiness.

Since I have been using Love Sparks successfully in my own life and with my clients since 2010, I have learned how to make them more accessible.

Love Sparks supercharged my relationship, and I want you to have a supercharged relationship, too!

Love Sparks rock!

You, too, can have a Relationship on Fire!

I invite you to strike the match!

Laying the Foundation for Love Sparks

"Habits are a type of learning. By forming a habit, the brain frees the mind to do other things without deliberation."

—**Benjamin Gardner,** Health Psychology
Lecturer at King's College, London

Love Sparks are *Good Relationship Habits* that I discovered when I investigated my own relationship and launched my Love Spark adventure.

It was a reasonably nice day, and I had some thoughts that I wanted to share with my spouse. I went into our bedroom and began talking about what was on my mind. I had some new ideas and plans for the future, so I was excited. He seemed to be listening but then he suddenly walked away and left me standing alone in the doorway as if I hadn't said anything. Was he dismissing me?

Was he ignoring me? At first, I was dumbfounded. I wasn't used to his being this way. He didn't usually do this.

But at that moment, I realized that I did.

Yes, I did. And I'm not proud of it, especially at that moment when he acted just like me. What I had to say seemed to be of no interest. He acted like he had better things to do. It was then that I realized what it must be like to deal with *me* sometimes. That wasn't a pleasant realization.

Have you noticed that you and your partner start to act in the same ways after years together? Most of the time, it's good. Like me, though, you might notice a Bad Relationship Habit of yours showing up in your partner. Don't worry, it isn't anything horrible. It's merely a process by which we grow to feel the same emotions. We're mimics. The longer and happier we are together, the more habits we share.

Every time a habit runs, it gets reinforced, much like hiking on a well-worn path. When there is a path, there is not much thought or energy expended on which way to go. You just go. However, when there is no path, it requires a lot of thought and energy to make the trip. The brain works in much the same way when it comes to habits.

That's why driving a stick shift, for example, becomes easy, even second nature, after some time. It becomes so routine that you may find yourself trying to find the clutch later when using an automatic transmission.

How often have you headed to the gym only to end up at the office or vice versa? Since I fly frequently, I sometimes end up heading to the airport when I meant to go to the grocery store. Habits have power. Developing new, *on-purpose* relationship habits (Love Sparks) results in a force that **supercharges** couples!

As reported in *ScienceDaily*, habits drive roughly 40 percent of everything we do every day. Imagine—40 percent! Forty percent of *everything* you do, *every day*, is driven by **habits**. This news is staggering for an individual, and when you add your partner, it creates new combinations of habits. Buried within these are the ones I refer to as Bad Relationship Habits. Everybody has them, and you will soon have an opportunity to discover yours.

Habits and the Brain

Your habits are not in the same part of your brain as willpower and decision-making. They're in the part of the brain that plays a vital role in the development of emotions, memories, and patterns. Since habits live here, once they're activated, you literally have no choice about it. The habit runs automatically every time it's triggered.

Willpower and decision-making (executive function) are in a different part of the brain altogether. Once you form a habit, this part of the brain gets left out. That means decisions are not useful for changing habits, and you cannot depend upon willpower alone. Trying really hard not to do something won't cut it. You will need an entirely different kind of approach if you want to break habits.

First, I will help you identify your habits and deconstruct them. Then, I will walk you through Love Sparks to transform them completely.

Habits Identified

The term *Bad Relationship Habit* might be a little confusing, so let's clear that up. Start by thinking of some everyday bad habits like:

- leaving clothes on the floor
- improperly squeezing a toothpaste tube

- failing to put the cap back on something
- leaving the toilet seat up
- cooking and leaving the dishes behind
- running late
- forgetting to pick up items
- failing to turn off the lights
- leaving the water running

If you were to change any or all of these habits, it would probably make a big difference in your relationship. Those kinds of habits, though, are not the kind I am referring to here. The ones I want to discuss are an entirely different type of habit: Bad Relationship Habits.

I'm referring to habits that show up in the form of *attitudes*, ways that you or your partner might act or be with one another. These habits can show up in *actions* like the common ones I previously listed, or they may not. You might ignore them because they are something you do silently, with a gesture or a look. You or your partner may dismiss them, saying, "I didn't do anything," "What's wrong with you?" or "What are you talking about?"

Here are some personal examples of my Bad Relationship Habits:

When I am in deep creative thought and get interrupted, especially by someone I love, that is a trigger. The behavior that follows might be a look, ignoring the person who interrupted me, even brushing them off. Or I might use sharp words to express my irritation. That's my behavior. The interruption is the trigger. I refer to this as "being a porcupine." The visual is that of needles pointing out, ready to defend myself.

For example, your partner says something to you in a particular way (perhaps a tone of voice), and you react. What they say and how they say it is a trigger and your reaction is the behavior. Most of your relationship habits are triggered by your partner, close friends, and your family members.

When my dad came home from work when I was a boy, I would hear the car pull into the driveway. That was a trigger that caused me to get dressed quickly and slip out the back door. If I didn't get out in time, my dad would have a to-do list for me the minute he walked in. Whatever was on his list wasn't anything I wanted to do.

I call this one my "escape" habit. Sometimes when Dad managed to corner me, he would question me. The questions were a prelude to his telling me what I needed to do before I could do anything else.

My "escape" habit still shows up in my life. Whenever my spouse asks me what is on my schedule, my brain will immediately go to "I'm being questioned." My body tenses up, ready for an escape. Of course, that is not what is happening, but it triggers the part of me that doesn't like being told what to do.

Your Turn

What is one of your Bad Relationship Habits? Do you know? If you have the courage, you could ask your partner, and they can likely tell you instantly. Another way is to consider what your partner complains about the most when it comes to your behavior. You can use the following list as a way to stimulate your thinking. It isn't essential to come up with the absolute right habit. You just need to think about one you can identify with.

Bad Relationship Habits include:

- being dismissive
- being aggressive
- being impolite

- being inappropriately loud
- acting superior
- putting your partner down verbally or otherwise
- giving your partner a certain "look"
- being passive-aggressive
- being easily annoyed
- being impatient
- being critical
- ignoring your partner
- being nasty
- shutting down
- being defensive
- giving your partner the cold shoulder or silent treatment (stonewalling)
- being condescending
- pretending to listen
- pointing the finger at your partner automatically when something goes bad
- dismissing your partner's thoughts, opinions, and ideas
- jumping to conclusions and then acting too quickly
- holding back
- yelling or screaming
- nagging
- running away
- over-compromising
- being bossy
- being a YES addict
- pleading
- projecting your shortcomings onto your partner
- tormenting
- rambling

- nit-picking
- criticizing
- making others the butt of jokes

Your Bad Relationship Habit may be on this list or you might come up with one of your own. One thing to know is that habits don't always seem to be bad. For example, you might be a pleaser, a YES addict, or overly friendly, and these can be Bad Relationship Habits, too. Choose one that fits you best, even if you are not entirely sure. You will be able to adjust it in the next section.

Your Bad Relationship Habit: _____

Understanding the Elements

Every habit starts with a psychological pattern and follows a particular sequence. The pattern consists of **four elements**:

- trigger
- behavior
- toll
- reward

Sometimes understanding these elements, each of which I'll explain, will help you see the habit. You'll want to understand these elements and use them to look deep within yourself, especially in terms of how they operate within a long-term relationship.

The First Element: Trigger

A **trigger** starts a series of reactions. It makes a connection in the brain that makes you do or act in some way. The environment can be a trigger. For instance, you might get triggered walking into a particular kind of room. Family members, friends, and your partner can all be triggers, too, and people are usually the key to most of your triggers when it comes to relationship habits. When you are around the same people doing the same things, the triggers will cause you to react the same way every time. Every time!

Consider these scenarios from my life:

1. After being gone a few days on a business trip, I arrive home and pull into my garage. The garage is a mess, and the messy garage is a **trigger** for me.
2. When I am in deep creative thought, I get interrupted. The interruption is a **trigger** for me.

Here are some examples of triggers that may apply to you:

- Someone speaks sharply to you.
- You are interrupted.
- You are confronted with conflict.
- Someone around you is unhappy.
- You are asked to do something.
- Someone wants your time.
- You get "the look."
- Someone grunts instead of making a statement.
- You feel dismissed.
- Your partner forgets something.
- Your partner is late.
- Your partner answers their phone or texts while you are talking.
- Someone is upset with you.
- Your partner flirts or shows attention to others.
- Your partner showboats.

- Your partner overspends or misuses money (in your opinion).
- Your partner pesters you.
- You're questioned about something.
- You're put on the spot.
- Others enter your personal space.
- You don't like the way your partner eats.
- The way your partner breathes bothers you.
- Your partner is impatient with you.
- Your partner rambles.
- Your partner tells horrible jokes or the same ones over and over.
- You feel embarrassed by what your partner does or says.
- Your space is a mess.
- You don't get your way.
- Someone expresses anger.

Write down one or two triggers that you believe are related to you and your Bad Relationship Habit.

_____

_____

The Second Element: Behavior

Behavior refers to the *action* of the habit, and it's relatively easy to identify. It's what you *do* after the trigger.

Let's take my scenarios one step further:

1. A messy garage is the **trigger.** The **behavior** is that I get upset, critical, and express my disapproval.
2. An interruption is a **trigger** for me. The **behavior** is that I get irritated and annoyed.

Review the following examples and see if you recognize any behaviors related to your Bad Relationship Habit. Do any of these seem familiar?

- You rush your partner.
- You express irritation.
- You ignore them.
- You ignore your responsibilities.
- You walk away.
- You brush off your partner.
- You dismiss them.
- You express disapproval.
- You put them down.
- You speak sharply.
- You are extra nice.
- You say "yes" no matter how you feel.
- You are rude or inconsiderate.
- You are overly attentive to your partner.
- You take on other people's emotions.

Write down one or two behaviors that relate to you and your Bad Relationship Habit.

_____

_____

The Third Element: Toll

A **toll** is a cost of some kind. Bad Relationship Habits take their toll. In fact, the cost is how you will know a good habit from a bad one. Let's add this to my scenarios:

1. The messy garage is a **trigger** for me. The **behavior** is that I get upset, critical, and express my disapproval. The **toll** is an immediate feeling of distance between my partner and me.
2. An interruption is a **trigger** for me. The **behavior** is that I get irritated and annoyed. The **toll** is that the feeling of love disappears between my partner and me.
3. Toll examples include:

    - emotional distance with your partner (or someone you love)
    - distraction
    - your partner (or others) feels insignificant around you
    - your partner (or others) feels they have no value around you
    - loss of affinity
    - loss of love
    - loss of intimacy
    - loss of self-respect or self-worth
    - isolation or loneliness
    - emotional stress
    - loss of overall well-being, health, or vitality
    - a sense of being trapped
    - hopelessness

Write down one or two tolls that relate to you and your Bad Relationship Habit.

_____

_____

The Fourth and Final Element: Reward

Bad Relationship Habits rarely, if ever, get us what we really want but we *are* getting something. The **reward** is what you ultimately get out of the behavior, and it's almost never easy to spot. As you examine your Bad Relationship Habit, spend some real time on it. Play around with it, sleep on it, and allow things to surface. Let it percolate until you see your reward. Ask those who are close to you to help in this exploration, if you wish.

Let's revisit those scenarios:

1. The messy garage is a **trigger** for me. The **behavior** is I get upset, critical, and express my disapproval. The **toll** is an immediate feeling of distance between my partner and me. The **reward** is that I'm in control, and I eventually get what I want: a clean garage.
2. An interruption is a **trigger** for me. The **behavior** is I get irritated and annoyed. The **toll** is that the feeling of love disappears between my partner and me. The **reward** is that I get to be left alone (not bothered) to do my own thing.

Some rewards you might get from your Bad Relationship Habits include:

- solitude
- admiration
- popularity
- appreciation
- attention
- feeling of superiority
- sense of control
- power
- recognition

- being perceived as smart
- getting out of responsibility
- getting your way
- winning
- getting out of perceived trouble
- hiding out
- doing what you want
- avoiding conflict

Write down one or two rewards that relate to you and your Bad Relationship Habit.

_____

_____

The Deconstruction Model

The more "parts" you can see of any habit or behavior give you more access to that habit or behavior. And that gives you the power to make changes.

Now that you have some idea of your Bad Relationship Habit and its elements, let me walk you through a couple of mine. Then you'll have the chance to deconstruct your own. My most obvious Bad Relationship Habits are that I am dismissive, and I am a "porcupine" who is easily annoyed.

Let me walk you through my Bad Relationship Habits from trigger to reward, while you consider your own.

Bad Relationship Habit #1: Dismissiveness

My triggers:

- My partner rambles.
- The conversation lacks relevancy.
- My partner continues to talk after the point has been made, or a conversation has ended.

My behaviors:

- I divert my attention.
- I go into my own thoughts.
- I treat my partner as though he isn't present.
- I become impatient.

The toll:

- My partner feels insignificant.
- My partner feels like he has no value.
- We lose connection and a sense of affinity, love, and intimacy.

My rewards:

- I am in control.
- I get to be left alone.
- I can do my own thing.

Bad Relationship Habit #2: Acting Like a Porcupine (Easily Annoyed)

My triggers:

- I am interrupted.

- My alone time is disturbed.
- My momentum gets disrupted.

My behaviors:

- I am sharp-tongued and hurtful.
- I give a disapproving or disgruntled look.
- I brush my partner off.

The toll:

- My partner feels insignificant.
- My partner feels like he has no value.
- We lose connection and a sense of affinity, love, and intimacy.

My rewards:

- I am in control.
- I get to be left alone.
- I can do my own thing.

After you've identified your own Bad Relationship Habits, complete the following:

My Bad Relationship Habits are:

_____

_____

_____

My triggers are:

_____

_____

_____

_____

My behaviors are:

_____

_____

_____

_____

The tolls (on my relationship, my partner, or myself) are:

_____

_____

_____

_____

My rewards are:

_____

_____

_____

_____

Once you've broken down these elements, you will likely gain many insights about your Bad Relationship Habits. The insights are exciting to see, but they only make a difference once you put them into action. **Love Sparks are those actions**.

The Do-Over Game

After I understood that I could be dismissive with my spouse, I worked very hard to force myself to stop it. "Play nice," I'd say to myself, but it didn't work. When my partner said something that would trigger my dismissiveness, I would stop listening and ignore him. To me, this is an offensive way to be with the one I love.

When I failed, I promised myself to get it right the next time, only to have it happen again. Of course it would. It's a habit, and willpower alone cannot help. Trying to do it right and be better with no structure is *a losing battle*.

One of the most successful games I want to introduce you to is called the Do-Over Game, and it's a fun way for you and your partner to support one other in disarming Bad Relationship Habits.

These are the rules:

1. **Both partners** must agree to the rules of the game and to participate *lovingly*.
2. If you happen to fall into your Bad Relationship Habit, ask for a Do-Over as soon as you notice. There is no need for excuses or apologies. Skip all of that and simply ask for the Do-Over.
3. When asked, the partner *must* accept and allow for the Do-Over.
4. The spirit of a Do-Over is to remain centered as a couple. Don't use it to act out or attack your partner.

Use the Do-Over game in the spirit of both of you winning and make it fun. Remember, your relationship partner is also your playmate. If that's become lost over the years, this game can bring it back. We all long for a deeper connection, especially with our partners.

Your Deepest Desire lies underneath these deconstructed Bad Relationship Habits. Your Deepest Desire is exceptional. It ties into every aspect of your life.

What's incredible and intriguing about your Deepest Desire is that it is also your most valuable **gift** to the world. We'll dig into that next.

Your Deepest Desire (Love Spark #1)

The announcement came over the PA system from the cockpit.

"Ladies and gentlemen, we are having some mechanical difficulties, and we will be landing in Seattle, Washington, for repairs. We apologize for the inconvenience and will have you back in the air as quickly as possible, then off to Honolulu, Hawaii."

SeaTac International Airport had cleared us for landing at 11:30 p.m. It was 1991, and I was flying to Hawaii for business. They took us off the airplane knowing that the repairs were going to take some time.

This will be my chance, I thought. I've got to do it. I've got to get his attention. But as we exited the airplane, I lost sight of him.

The airport was completely dark except for the waiting area, and I looked everywhere but couldn't find him. I was about to give up when I heard his voice in my head: "It is in your moments of decision that your destiny is shaped."

And then finally, I saw him: Tony Robbins and his wife. They were on the same flight but in first class. It was pretty exciting knowing he was on the airplane. I was in coach, and before we were forced to land, I was going nuts trying to figure out how in the world I was going to talk to him. The forced landing created the perfect opportunity. I wanted him to know the difference he had made in my life, and the opportunities that had opened up because of him.

In 1987, I read *Unlimited Power*, his first bestseller. My job performance improved, and I began hitting levels previously beyond my reach. I was promoted and the company transferred me to Los Angeles, California. I didn't even know I wanted to live in California and I've now been here for thirty years.

As I walked toward Robbins and his wife, slowly but deliberately, I became more and more nervous. I thought, what if I can't say anything? What if my throat closes off? The forty yards or so between us seemed endless. At long last, I was face-to-face with him.

"Mr. Robbins," I said sheepishly.

He was every way you would hope he might be: open, enthusiastic, and genuinely happy that I found him.

"I won't take much of your time," I said, "but I wanted to thank you and let you know the enormous difference your book has made in my life."

He gave me a wide grin.

I shook his hand, and as I was about to leave, completely happy, he asked, "Do you have a card?"

"Yes," I replied, and I handed him my card.

He said, "I'll send you a signed copy of my newest book."

Wow! This was so far beyond what I had hoped for.

"Thank you again," I said. "And thank you, Becky, for allowing me to intrude."

She smiled, and I walked away.

Most of us want to feel like we make a difference in this world. It doesn't need to be profound. You just want to have a sense that your life matters. You want to believe that you have something to contribute: a valuable skill, knowledge, or experience. You want those whom you care about to be better and richer because you are in their lives.

Listen to Your Heart

Achieving these things is very important, but they can still leave you with a craving. A craving that is left unfulfilled most of the time. What you crave is your *Deepest Desire*, and it is nestled *underneath* the reward of your Bad Relationship Habits.

You have been trying to satisfy your Deepest Desire through the people around you. When they could not fulfill it, you unconsciously developed Bad Relationship Habits. Everyone does it. Making it their fault seems like a natural consequence of your expectations not being met.

The only place your Deepest Desire resides is in your heart, not your head. That's where you will find what you are genuinely looking for. Focusing on your innermost self is key, and until you ask the right questions, you will continue to look for the answers in the wrong places.

How do you do this?

Sit quietly and try to get in touch with your feelings.

What do you desire?

What do you ache for?

What do you yearn for?

Listen to your heart.

It will open, little by little, as you go deeper and deeper.

What do you desire? What do you ache for? What do you yearn for?

Is it to be heard? Seen as you really are? To feel unconditionally loved?

I ask you again: What do you desire? What do you ache for? What is the yearning of your heart?

Is it to be completely accepted? Understood? Paid attention to?

I ask you again: What do you desire? What do you ache for? What do you yearn for?

Is it freedom? Is it to be peaceful? To have peace of mind and enjoy a loving, relaxing environment?

I ask you again: What do you desire? What do you ache for? What is the yearning of your heart?

Is it to know who you really are, beyond your ego-self and its cravings? Is it to know your higher self and its connection to all that is? Is it to be appreciated and acknowledged?

I ask you one last time: What do you desire? What do you ache for? What do you yearn for?

What is your Deepest Desire?

What is deeper than anything you can find beneath the ego, beneath your personality?

Your Deepest Desire may be:

- peace, peacefulness, peace of mind
- to be loved deeply
- fearlessness
- an open heart
- a sense of belonging

- extreme connection
- feeling cherished
- appreciation
- respect
- to be known as you really are
- acceptance
- to be heard
- unconditional love
- attention
- understanding
- to be acknowledged/noticed
- to really matter

Choose one from the list that rings most true for you and say it out loud. (It can always be adjusted later.)

Then, write it down.

My Deepest Desire is _____

How does it feel? Does it feel like it fits for you? Does it move you in some way or tug at your heart? You're about to test your Deepest Desire, and you will need your Bad Relationship Habit reward from Chapter One to do that.

Write down your Bad Relationship Habit reward here:

_____

Now, consider these questions and the following examples:

1. What does your reward *protect* you from?
2. What does your reward *provide* for you emotionally?
3. What can your reward be considered a *substitute* for?

Here are my answers:

- My reward (being left alone) protects me from feelings of chaos and difficulty.
- My reward (being left alone) gives me a sense of control when peace seems impossible.
- My reward (being left alone) is a substitute for being peaceful.
- My Deepest Desire is to be peaceful.

Here are my spouse's answers, based on his own Bad Relationship Habit. He can be judgmental, and his rewards are feeling superior and smart.

- His reward (superiority) protects him from feeling vulnerable and looking stupid.
- His reward (superiority) gives him a sense of control and worth.
- His reward (superiority) is a substitute for approval.
- His Deepest Desire is for approval.

Here is how my dear friend Melodye answered these questions. Her Bad Relationship Habit is to hold back her love. Her reward is being in control.

- Her reward protects her from feeling hurt.
- Her reward lets her feel safe emotionally.
- Her reward is a substitute for feeling loved unconditionally.
- Melodye's Deepest Desire is to feel loved unconditionally.

Here's another example. This is how my dear friend JoAnne answered these questions. Her Bad Relationship Habit is to beg for acknowledgment. Her reward is that she feels like she matters and is worth fighting for.

- Her reward protects her from feeling left out.
- Her reward is that she feels emotionally connected.
- Her reward is a substitute for feeling cherished.
- Jo Anne's Deepest Desire is to feel cherished.

Here are the questions again, ready for your responses:

1. What does your reward protect you from?

_____

_____

2. What does your reward provide for you emotionally?

_____

_____

3. What can your reward be a substitute for?

_____

_____

Does the Deepest Desire you chose match the answer to the third question? If not, take another look at the list of Deepest Desires and repeat the exercise choosing a different one.

How Do You Satisfy Your Deepest Desire?

Good question. You fulfill your Deepest Desire by expressing it. It might sound counterintuitive, but you cannot have it unless you find a way to "give it away."

It's not only your Deepest Desire, but it is also your gift to the world. It's how you make a difference, how you feel like you matter, and how you make the lives of others richer and better. **Your Deepest Desire is your Unique Contribution.**

As author and motivational speaker Zig Ziglar put it, "You can get what you really want if you just help enough other people get what they want."

Action Steps

Here are some examples of how to "give away" your Deepest Desire and how to make it your Unique Contribution:

- If your Deepest Desire is peace of mind, then be someone who provides peace of mind for your partner and others.
- If your Deepest Desire is approval, then show approval for your partner and others.
- If your Deepest Desire is unconditional love, then love your partner and others unconditionally.
- If your Deepest Desire is to feel cherished, then make certain your partner and others feel cherished.

Find at least **five ways** to do this every day. Don't sleep tonight until you've accomplished this. Then do it again tomorrow (and the next day and the next) until it becomes your new habit.

Giving Away Your Deepest Desire

Whatever you chose as your Deepest Desire is perfect. As you practice giving it away and move through the book, this habit will become more refined and you'll find many different ways to express it. With a partner or on your own, discovering this Love Spark will raise all of your relationships to a new level.

Now you have an understanding of why you do some of the things you do. Also, you have an understanding of what you are really after.

You can give your Deepest Desire to others in any relationship or none at all. There's something else to ask yourself.

How do the things you care about influence whom you choose for a partner and whom you don't? Do you really know *why* you want a relationship anyway? Let's consider that next.

Fill in the Blanks

Love Spark #1: My Unique Contribution
(Giving Away My Deepest Desire)

My Bad Relationship Habit reward is _____

_____

My Deepest Desire is _____

_____

Why? (Love Spark #2)

I was listening to a speaker in a room of about one hundred people when I suddenly said to myself, as though talking to a stranger, "I am living my life like I am already dead."

You see, I had had a partner for about sixteen years, and none of those years were bad ones. We had love, but the relationship was missing everything else I really wanted. Year after year, I tried to make the relationship into what it never *was*, and on this day, I realized it never *could be*.

Ouch! Sixteen years! I led and participated in many self-improvement programs over that period, and I worked on that relationship in every one of them. I was certain I could transform it and that it could be what I wanted and needed. We had everything except chemistry. And you can't sidestep chemistry. It's either there or it's not.

Why did I stay in this relationship for such a long time? It was familiar, and it was comfortable. My partner provided a lot for me and loving him was easy. Plus, I traveled extensively for my work so I got to do my own thing without having to reconcile my time.

That was my *Why*. And on this day, as I sat in that classroom, I saw the cost. He deserved to have someone who loved him for more than just familiarity and comfort. It was on that note that we ended our relationship, as we knew it. Because of the many years we spent together, we parted as family. And to this day we are there for each other as brothers and always will be.

Asking the Question

Before that time, I had never drilled down to *why* I wanted to be in a relationship.

I never asked what I really wanted and needed in a partner. Nor did I think about my deal-breakers and where I was willing to compromise.

Over the years, I've asked this question of every couple with whom I've worked. Why are you in this relationship? If you are not in one, then why do you want one? I am assuming that you are in a relationship or want a relationship because you are reading this book. *But why?*

Very rarely do people have a clearly defined response to that question. You might not either, at least not at this moment. That's not a problem, provided you are willing to examine it. Knowing your Why lets you access more of what you want in *any* relationship.

The best relationships are not by luck, accident, or fate. They exist because those in the relationship know *why* they are in them. Knowing *why* gives you a contextual view for having the relationship work.

There are several steps to answering Why. The first step is understanding how relationships happen.

Cocktails Anyone?

Let me introduce you to the first stage of love. It is where love *feels* the most real and where the "love cocktail" gets mixed. This "cocktail" gives you the experience of a full and meaningful bond that can include a romantic surge (with a twist of hope).

The cocktail is a mixture of hormones, which are natural drugs that get released in your body. These hormones can lead to sex, but they won't usually build a lasting relationship. Because of that, I call this stage "H.I.G.H.":

- **H**ighly
- **I**ntoxicated
- **G**iddy
- **H**appy

Stage One is all biology, hormones, and chance. It is a euphoric period filled with romance and intimacy. Your heart orders the brain to mix up the cocktail and that leads to the pitter-patter of your emotions.

During this stage:

- You miss and desire each other often.
- You and your new love play up your similarities.
- You play down your differences.
- Your inhibitions are lowered while your level of trust is heightened.
- You have more energy, and you require less sleep.

Beyond the biology of a relationship, why do you want it? When you come down from the effects of the "love cocktail," what then? It might seem like something went wrong. Often couples without the "cocktail" feel like the relationship is failing. Can love survive? And if it can, how?

Logically, you know that high can't last forever. Logic doesn't matter, though, because emotionally you are stuck in the hope that it will last forever. I think that was me. I thought once in love, that high should last forever. When I look back now, I can see how I chased love and tried to freeze it in time. Have you ever done that? It's a terrible waste of energy.

Having a companion for a lifetime requires that you move through the early stages of love. That involves experiencing and enjoying them for sure, but then moving to what the later stages can make available. And that is love and intimacy without the influence of the hormone cocktail. It's uncharted territory for any new couple, but a lifetime of "true love" requires that you move into this unknown. You don't want to get stuck in one place or one experience.

The new normal will be to keep the experience of love alive beyond the hormones and becoming a Partner for Life. A Partner for Life is being a partner who is more interested in how much "aliveness" they can bring to each other. That means that your partner—being with you—has more life, more happiness, and more peace.

Conditions of Satisfaction

I trained for a decade with Patricia McDade, an amazing coach and teacher, and her staff. I've had the privilege of many great teachers over the years, and she was the best.

She trained me in a set of principles called *Conditions of Satisfaction*, which I'd like to share with you. I found these principles essential in getting to the Why of relationships. You can use them to get to the Why of your relationship or any relationship that you might want. Getting to your Why will provide the basis for learning and practicing Love Sparks—and get you to **a supercharged Relationship on Fire**!

To get to your Conditions of Satisfaction, you must first brainstorm everything that you would ever want in a partner. Don't focus on your current partner. Instead, think about what you want in a partner for life to achieve your dreams. You don't have to break up with your current partner if they don't match your list. Just go with the exercise for the sake of the exercise itself and trust the process. More will be revealed as you progress. Getting to your Why is all you are after right now.

One friend of mine who did this exercise wrote about sixty items on her list. WOW! She was really specific. Write down as many as you can, as long as they apply to *your* tastes. Nothing is written in stone, and everything can be changed. Just get the ones that seem important to you down on paper.

To help you prime the pump and stimulate your thinking, here is my list:

- I want someone who is my height, tight and lean.
- I want someone who has a high regard for our quality of life.
- I want somebody who's peaceful, harmonious, and adventurous.
- I want someone who is healthy and vital.
- I want someone who's focused on learning and growing.
- I want someone who is financially stable on their own.
- I want someone who already has children because I'm family-oriented and don't have any of my own.
- I want someone who loves to travel with me.
- I want someone who enjoys socializing with me.

- I want someone with whom I enjoy being intimate and who enjoys being intimate with me.
- I want someone who enjoys and works toward a pristine home.
- I want someone who loves to be with me but is independent and perfectly content doing his own thing in his own space while also honoring mine.
- I want someone who honors my family, who they are for me, and who they are for us as a couple.
- I want someone who respects my work, my career, and my hobbies, not at the expense of his own but because I like to be busy. That won't change, so I need someone willing to embrace that.

Take the time now and start making your list. Return to the book once you have at least twenty items or so. **Don't skip this step.** It sets up everything for the rest of the book. Also, try not to judge your answers. You can refine them later.

My Conditions of Satisfaction:

_____
_____
_____
_____
_____
_____
_____
_____

Take your list and review your Conditions of Satisfaction, answering these two questions for each condition:

1. If you didn't have this condition fulfilled, how would it affect you?
2. Could you live without it?

Remove the conditions that you can live without. Just for now, remove or move them to the bottom of your list. You could even make a "not now" list, if you like.

Here's an example from my list: *I want someone who enjoys and works toward a pristine home.* Though this is important to me, it didn't make it to the top. There are other items on my list that matter more to me.

Go through your list again. This time ask yourself which ones *absolutely* need to stay. You might even rate them in the order of importance, if that helps. The goal here is to get to the conditions that you absolutely must have. You might need to do this step a few times.

I narrowed my list down to:

- I want somebody who's peaceful, harmonious, and adventurous.
- I want someone who has his own money and is financially stable.
- I want someone who enjoys social interaction, travel, and intimacy with me.
- I want someone who honors my family, who they are for me, and who they are for us as a couple.
- I want someone who loves to be with me but is independent and perfectly content doing his own thing in his own space while also honoring mine.

As I went through my list, I checked in with myself and set my top Conditions of Satisfaction. The others are also important to me, but if I have these, then I am willing to compromise on the others.

Rise to the Top

A beautiful consequence of this exercise that might surprise you is your ability and willingness to compromise. I have found that I'm happy when those conditions not at the top of my list only get fulfilled some of the time. It isn't that they aren't important. It's just the realization and acceptance that it is unlikely that one person will fulfill every item on my list, all of the time. You'll find it is easy to compromise when your most important desires get fulfilled *most of the time*. The partner who does that is a keeper.

Once you have your five to seven top Conditions of Satisfaction, you will see something unexpected that will help uncover the reason why you want a relationship.

My Why became clear rather quickly. I read through my top desires and gave myself time to sit and be with them. I thought about each one. And as I thought about them collectively, this is what I realized: I want a relationship because I want a *companion* for a variety of reasons (socializing, travel, intimacy).

If you were to ask me why I have a relationship, my answer so far would be, "I have a relationship because I want a life companion. Someone with whom I feel peaceful, financially secure, and can be with socially and all that that includes."

Taking into account the work you did in the last chapter, you might remember that peace of mind is what I found to be my Deepest Desire. Being peaceful is also my ultimate Why response. The response to my Why fulfills my Deepest Desire for peace of mind and a peaceful environment. For me, companionship and financial security equal peace. Enjoying a partner who likes intimacy with me also provides peaceful security.

Don't skip anything here. Are your top Conditions of Satisfaction laid out, at least for now? Refer to your Deepest Desire from the exercise in Chapter Two. I hope you are committing that to memory. Apply it to each of your top Conditions of Satisfaction, as I do here.

My Deepest Desire is: To be peaceful/have peace of mind

My top Conditions of Satisfaction:

A companion who's peaceful, harmonious, and adventurous. Does this fulfill my Deepest Desire for peace of mind?

A companion who has his own money and is financially stable. Does this fulfill my Deepest Desire for peace of mind?

A companion who enjoys social interaction, travel, and intimacy (all of these with me). Does this fulfill my Deepest Desire for peace of mind?

A companion who honors my family and who they are for me and who they are for our relationship. Does this fulfill my Deepest Desire for peace of mind?

A companion who loves to be with me and is independent and perfectly content doing his own thing, having his own space, and honoring mine. Does this fulfill my Deepest Desire for peace of mind?

I answered "yes" to all of these. I feel solid and grounded that this is true for me. These constitute my Why, which is consistent with my Deepest Desire, and my Conditions of Satisfaction bear that out.

Now it's your turn.

My Deepest Desire from Chapter Two: _____

My TOP Conditions of Satisfaction:

_____

_____

_____

_____

Do your Conditions of Satisfaction fulfill your Deepest Desire? Do you say "yes" to all of yours?

Keep your Why in the forefront of your mind. *Making that a habit* will shape how you interact with people. It will help you determine who is the best fit for you. If you are in a partnership, you may now view your partner differently. Knowing *why* makes being in a relationship easier and more fulfilling. Do you see your Deepest Desire is also your ultimate Why?

A Couple's Why

For a couple to have harmony, the Whys need to dance together. If you are single, understanding yourself this way will make it easier to choose a future partner. Knowing both of your Why responses allows you to include all facets of your personalities.

Any two Whys can coexist. One is not better than another. When I understood that my spouse's Why is approval, it gave me new insight. His Bad Relationship Habit is being judgmental. I now have room for that, too. I can accept his Bad Relationship Habit as we work on developing Love Sparks.

I am very fortunate that my spouse fulfills everything on my list *some* of the time. And the top six *most* of the time. If you are in a relationship, this may not be the case for you. What you have learned about yourself may open up some new conversations. Together, you may see a lot of possibilities.

Congratulations on uncovering your Why!

Your ultimate answer to the question "Why a relationship?" is tied to your Deepest Desire.

Why is what gives you the courage to move through the tough spots of being a couple. This is what it takes to play the long game.

Love Spark #2 is keeping your Why in the forefront of your mind.

Many things can get in the way of what you really care about. Remembering your Why will help you get out of your own way to experience true love and the intimacy you really want.

What if I told you that hiking up a mountain and watching a movie would open up the next Love Spark? Let's see what these two activities have in common with reaching the next level on your journey to supercharging your relationship. (Don't worry, I climbed the mountain, so you don't have to.)

Fill in the Blanks

Love Spark #1: My Unique Contribution (Giving Away My Deepest Desire): _____

_____

Love Spark #2: My Response to Why (It Is Also My Deepest Desire): _____

_____

Letting Go of Judgment (Love Spark #3)

San Bruno Mountain sits in front of my house. It is a huge mountain that offers many hiking paths, and on this day my partner and I were hiking our favorite route.

How did we get there? This is how it started: I was in my office writing and took a break. I asked my partner if he wanted to hike once I finished for the day. His afternoon was open, the weather was spectacular, so he said he would.

Later, when we started up the hillside, he carried a pair of clippers and tongs. I noticed it but didn't ask why he brought those along. It wouldn't be long, though, before I found out. As we climbed, he started cutting limbs and weeds, grooming the path.

This wasn't the hike I had in mind or looked forward to. It wasn't the way we had ever hiked before. After all, this was going to be a ninety-minute trip, and I intended to go back to my writing as soon as we returned. With the unplanned gardening, it would take much longer. I noticed myself getting annoyed.

Expecting that he would not be far behind, I left him and started up the hill. Not long after, I realized he wasn't close at all. His path-grooming was a bigger project than I realized. My mind started racing. I thought about how I loved him but wanted him to be different than he was right then. I accept him mostly, but at that moment, I judged him. I thought he should be walking with me and not working on the path. This was *our* time to be together. In that moment of judgment and rejection, love was not present.

Being Together

Later that night, while we watched a movie, I had my writing in front of me and I was working on some edits. I immediately noticed that he paused the movie. I said, "Don't pause, I'm good." He told me no, he would wait for me.

"No," I said, "There is no need for that. I am good."

He said, "If you are going to work, I would prefer you not be here. I thought this was our time to be together."

"Yes," I said, "I want to be with you."

He replied, "Well, that's not how it feels to me."

Funny, this sounded familiar. Isn't this a double standard? I thought. Isn't that exactly what happened in the afternoon?

On my way to being annoyed again, I stopped. Wait! He wants to be with me, and I'm judging him. I am on the receiving end of what happened earlier in the day.

I realized that my judgment was replacing the experience of true love. It's clear the two cannot coexist, no matter how creative I think I am or how right I think I am. True love, the experience of love, is what really matters to me.

I reminded myself of our Deepest Desires: approval (his) and peace of mind (mine).

I put my writing away, I let go of my judgment, and was totally present with him as we watched the movie.

Is This True Love?

The topic of true love has been debated for centuries and probably will continue for many more. This chapter is not intended to further that debate, but rather to lay the foundation for your next Love Spark.

Whenever I've had the opportunity to talk to individuals about love, it almost always ends up on true love. It's rarely a fluid conversation. Instead, it's clunky and a little off-kilter because it's so conceptual.

Most of our notions about true love we get from television, movies, music, and books. They are beautiful ideas that fill us with mystery and romance, but they are hardly the day-to-day experiences of a loving couple. In fact, thinking that these notions represent reality can steer many relationships off course.

As I mentioned in the previous chapter, the initial biological attraction might get confused for true love. The experience, commonly known as "falling in love," is terrific because it is the best all-natural drug cocktail on the planet. With the right combination of stimuli, the heart signals the brain to flood the system with oxytocin and vasopressin. This gives an experience of being high along with a sense of well-being. In some cases, *falling in love* is the beginning of a long-term relationship, but it is not to be confused with *true love*.

Perhaps it would be easier if we looked at love in two ways: love and true love.

Dr. Gerald Jampolsky, author of *Love Is Letting Go of Fear*, makes what I see as this case: Love Is. It does not need you and it does not need me to exist, and that is the miracle.

True love, on the other hand, requires you and me. Think about it much like air. The air surrounds us but we won't experience it unless we breathe it in. By the same token, you must express *love* in order to experience *true love*. Keeping these two concepts distinct in your mind will help with the development of your next Love Spark.

The couples with whom I've worked tell me that after identifying true love, they had a greater experience of love for longer periods of time. I am convinced that we all want true love, if we want love at all. While not mistaking falling in love for true love, let us also not discount the blood, sweat, and tears that it takes for you to develop it for yourselves. Knowing that a relationship can be easier and more natural makes bringing true love into your life very enticing.

So then, what is *true love* exactly?

True love is the experience that your partner is perfect precisely the way they are and allowing them to be that way is a conscious decision.

True love acceptance is not the same as when we were under the influence of the hormone cocktail (the natural drug). It does not leave one feeling high but relatively peaceful, secure, and united.

Allowing one another to be as you are is how to experience true love. It is this moment-by-moment choice that sets the stage for Love Spark #3.

Easier Said than Done

I can tell you from my own experience, and from those to whom I've spoken on the subject, this is not easy. Simple, yes, but not easy.

The Bad Relationship Habit automatically runs *every single time* it's triggered. You have no choice about it. Remember, our habits get processed in one area of the brain and our willpower in another. Willpower is not involved in a Bad Relationship Habit.

Trying to change people or resisting how they are is a Bad Relationship Habit that we learn early on. It is so automatic that it might be hard to consider not doing. It might even seem so natural that you don't notice it happening. This habit is an internal conversation that takes place in your own head.

A judgment dialogue sounds something like this:

"If they would just . . ."
"There is no way I can be happy until they . . ."
"It would be better if they could . . ."

These are triggers for *resisting* how people are and *fighting* the way your partner is. It's a dialogue where you make yourself the judge.

As the judge, though, you create a toll, or a cost, for running this Bad Relationship Habit. The very thing you want most, your Deepest Desire, gets sacrificed. You cannot have it both ways. You cannot be the judge *and* fulfill your Deepest Desire. Sorry, but that's the way it is.

My Deepest Desire is peace of mind. How in the heck do I tie peace of mind to allowing others to be the way they are? Here's how:

Write your Deepest Desire here: _____

_____

Now, answer the following questions:

1. Does trying to change my partner (or anyone) fulfill my Deepest Desire?
2. When I feel others trying to change me, does that fulfill my Deepest Desire?

No and no! Both scenarios *isolate* you from others with judgment. Allowing your partner to be the way they are is a Love Spark. Letting go of judgment gives you the power to be the way you are, too.

Connection through Acceptance

Letting go of judging someone does not mean that you agree with them. Letting go of judging your partner and others is a way of accepting them and experiencing the Love Spark. Since judging is something we do automatically, it might seem impossible to stop. However, like any habit, you can stop through practice.

If you want to fulfill your Deepest Desire, it is *essential* that your communication with your partner and others allows for a sense of connection. You can achieve that desired connection through acceptance and by letting go of judgment.

Most of us are constantly judging. We judge our partners, ourselves, everybody. We also tend to look at others with a narrow mindset. We see only a piece of what's going on with them. When many of us were growing up, a lot of emphasis was put on "constructive criticism" that resulted in constant correction and judgment. So we tend to notice faults and differences instead of merit and similarities. We aren't bad people; we just have a Bad Relationship Habit.

Consider my hiking anecdote. I was annoyed that my spouse cleared the path while hiking with me. I thought it was a double standard that he could do path maintenance while on our hike but I couldn't edit during our movie. However, my desire to have love present superseded that thinking.

If you do not let go, then the price you pay is your Deepest Desire. Our Deepest Desire is what drives everything. If you trade having it fulfilled for being right about something, you become a prisoner of that judgment.

Letting go of judgment is possible. The Bad Relationship Habit will lose its grip as it becomes apparent that it simply cannot give you what you truly want.

Let go of words that:

- **categorize** you or your partner
- **measure or evaluate** you or your partner
- **judge or condemn** you or your partner

There is an added benefit, a miracle even, when you can create this experience. Allowing your partner to be as they are, you also discover *yourself*. You develop a capacity for experiencing your "true self," beyond the ego. You create a relationship where you can grow as an individual, and this ability alters *all* your relationships.

This Love Spark is to accept your partner by Letting Go of Judgment.

When I am free to be myself with my spouse, I experience that freedom everywhere. My heart is full and letting go becomes natural and easy. Can you feel the rawness of your heart? Can you feel your heart opening?

The heart is central to the emotional body and is a fascinating part of being human. It is the foundation of our next Love Spark.

Fill in the Blanks

Love Spark #1: My Unique Contribution (Giving Away My Deepest Desire): _____

_____

Love Spark #2: My Response to Why (It Is Also My Deepest Desire): _____

_____

Love Spark #3: Letting Go of Judgment

Stop! Look! Listen! (Love Spark #4)

> "There are many dimensions to listening.
> One is just like the sky: to be still and receive."
>
> —**Arjuna Ardagh,** author of *Better Than Sex*

The defining moment in my life came and went in a flash, but its impact was monumental.

What I wanted at the time was a cocktail before boarding my flight, a smooth touchdown in beautiful Cancun, and the person I loved most. It was 1993, and JP and I were celebrating nine years together.

My birthday was approaching, and he asked, "What do you want for your birthday?"

"Mexico, I want to go to Mexico!" I said.

Don't get me wrong, I know how entitled that might sound,

but it was said in a sea of exhaustion. I had always been a workaholic, which JP loved about me, but we both knew it was the one thing that came between us. I found it hard to tear myself away from my work. I could see it was testing us, and now we had an opportunity to get away from it all, just the two of us, and I wasn't going to pass it up.

"Mexico. You got it," he said. It was as simple as that. A chance for us to be together, without distractions, without telephone interruptions, and no missing romantic dinners because of business. It was going to be our time, and I was more than ready to board that plane.

I did have one more birthday wish, though it was not the most traditional gift you would expect.

"I want to get tested for HIV, both of us," I told him.

There was a moment of silence. I had caught JP off guard. I could see the cogs turning in his head, looking for the right response.

"I just think it's time we get checked," I said, trying to reassure him. "We have always practiced safe sex, and if we do this now, we have nothing to worry about."

We were standing in the middle of the kitchen, holding hands and staring into each other's eyes. A small grin appeared at the side of his mouth, and he finally replied, "If that is what you want, let's do it." And we did.

We arranged our flight to leave on my birthday, and two weeks later, we sat in the doctor's office.

"Which of you is Thomas?" he asked.

"I am," I said.

"You're negative," he told me. And for an instant, I was relieved.

But all of a sudden, I realized that his face was empty, and it frightened me. It was only seconds but it seemed like hours before he looked directly at JP.

"You're positive," the doctor said.

Hearing the news, my throat ran dry, my mind went completely dark, and I became numb. Nine months later, on Thanksgiving Day, JP passed away at twenty-nine years old.

I was heartbroken.

Heart*aches* and Heart*breaks*

For centuries, we've heard about the heart in a myriad of ways beyond its physical ability to pump blood through our bodies. We've heard:

- My **heart** aches for that family.
- I am broken-**heart**ed about it.
- Our **heart**s are filled with joy over the birth of our baby.
- She died from a broken **heart.**
- My **heart** was filled with love hearing them exchange vows.

When you're in a couple and you express your love, what you are communicating is beyond words. The two of you offer up your hearts to each other and say, "My heart is in your hands and I trust you with it." This gives room for both of you to be open, honest, and vulnerable.

Imagine if you showed up on the third date and said, "Be sure to call me. I'll feel abandoned if you don't call every day." Or imagine if your date said, "Be careful and please don't raise your voice with me. It will scare me and I will run away."

We don't feel comfortable saying things like that with a new love prospect, so we don't.

We don't say, "By the way, my heart comes with many wounds, emotional wounds that show up as tender spots and that are left behind by heart*aches* and heart*breaks* from my past." But that doesn't mean we don't feel it.

Tender Spots versus Emotional Wounds

Let's take a moment and differentiate the meanings of heart*ache* and heart*break*. We tend to use them both as though they are the same, but they impact us very differently. The next Love Spark will require that you know the difference.

Heart*ache* is caused by an emotional incident that leaves an ache, a tender spot if you will, within the emotional body. That tender spot will usually take care of itself on its own. In a relatively short period of time, it will disappear. It won't significantly impact the daily activities of your life.

Here's an example of heart*ache*:

My brother Eddie and I are in the back seat of my dad's 1963 Chevrolet Impala, and we're looking out the back window sadly as we drive away from the only home we've ever known. We're moving. We're moving away from our big cherry tree and all the things we knew to a new home in a subdivision. Our new backyard is bare, no trees, no grass, and all of our neighbors have fenced-in yards. It's a cookie-cutter house, a different school, a strange environment, and that is heart*ache* for two little kids.

I remember it took some encouragement from our parents to join activities where we made new friends. It wasn't long after we got settled into our new place and new school that the heart*ache* naturally passed. Most heart*aches* take care of themselves.

Can you think of any heart*aches* from your life? What comes to mind?

Write them down here:

_____

_____

_____

Notice that heart*aches* have minimal impact on your current experience of life and on your existing relationships. A heart*ache* is much like hitting a key on a piano; the tone lingers and before long it fades away. That's the nature of a heart*ache*.

Heart*breaks* are different. A heart*break* is different because it leaves an emotional wound. Unlike tender spots left by heart*ache*, this emotional wound runs much deeper. You will likely feel the effects of it in your existing and future relationships. It can be triggered repeatedly over the course of your entire life.

My story, as you came into this chapter, represented a heart*break*. When JP's results came back positive, my world crumbled and I felt dead inside. I felt betrayed, I couldn't move, I couldn't speak, and nine months later, he died. I was heart*broken*. This feeling gets triggered when my current spouse does anything where I think he could get hurt. He will sometimes get on the roof to clean the gutters. While he is perfectly capable, when I see him climb that ladder, my emotional wound gets triggered. That's the nature of heart*break*.

Another heart*break* example: I was about four years old, and I was next door at my best friend Bobby's house. They were about to lay a new sewer line so there was a massive ditch in their backyard. That muddy ditch was inviting for little boys, and we were having a blast out there playing in it. All of a sudden, I felt a great big hand grab me by my neck then jerk me up into his arms. He pulled my pants down and started spanking my bare butt as he walked us up the hill toward our house. It was my dad, and as I looked out, I could see Bobby, his father, and all my friends looking up in disbelief. I was humiliated and embarrassed for the first time ever, *and* my dad wouldn't listen to me! I wanted to tell him Bobby's dad said it was okay.

You see, before my dad had left for work, he saw me looking at that ditch.

"Son, don't go in that ditch," he said. "It could be dangerous."

"Okay," I agreed.

Later, when Bobby invited me, I told him I couldn't because my dad told me not to.

His dad chimed in, though, and said, "Don't worry about it, Little T, it'll be fine. I'm gonna be right here with you."

With his permission, I ran to the ditch and played. When dad grabbed me, I was heart*broken,* not because of the humiliation or even the embarrassment, but because my dad wouldn't listen to me. He wouldn't let me explain. That was the heart*break.* To this day, that heart*break* gets triggered whenever I feel misunderstood or unable to explain myself, especially with my spouse.

Explore some of your heart*breaks* and notice how they linger and often trigger your Bad Relationship Habits. As you think of them now, you may even feel the emotional weight of them. Don't get stuck with that weight, but I do want you to notice how it feels.

Please start a short list of your heart*breaks.*

_____

_____

_____

Are you experiencing the nature of a heart*break*? Can you feel the tug on your emotions as you revisit yours? They hang around, and they influence a lot of your decisions, especially regarding relationships. You might not realize it, but they do. There is a natural tendency to resist the experience of emotional pain.

Don't Resist the Pain

You cannot resist your pain and fulfill your Deepest Desire at the same time. When it comes to a special relationship, an intimate one, your partner will eventually hit those emotional wounds. They can't help it. It will be unintentional, and they will likely not even know what happened. The truth is, you may not know what's happened either.

If you use the same metaphor I applied to a heart*ache*, hitting a key on the piano, the heart*break* key gets pounded harder and plays multiple times throughout your lifetime. When you are falling in love, though, the "love cocktail" makes the heart*breaks* temporarily disappear. You know they are there at some level, but they have no power because you are on a natural high.

And this is where it gets interesting.

You and your partner trust each other with your hearts, and the relationship expands while the "love cocktail" loses its grip. Then you both stumble upon those emotional wounds, activating the pain and triggering your Bad Relationship Habits.

How do you do that? *Why* do you do that?

We are going to address both the how and why together. It just so happens that your partner is the perfect person to provoke memories that will hit those emotional wounds imprinted on your heart. Those memories are stored in the same part of the brain as habits, so when that emotional wound gets hit, it's as though the heart*break* incident of the past is happening again in the present.

Getting to the Love Spark

We may live our lives moment by moment, but we view our time as a fluid, continuous line. I call that the *Timeline Life*. It looks like this: You're born, and there's this long line (we hope), and then you die.

To have real power over your emotional wounds, you want to get really good at shifting from the Timeline Life to the *Right-Now-Life*. Within those *moment-by-moment* moments, the Right-Now-Life, the possibility of fulfilling your Deepest Desire, becomes very real.

How do you shift from the Timeline Life experience, where everything blurs together, to the Right-Now-Life experience?

Slow down and let go of your reactions.

Let go as much as you can *without resisting anything*, and take these three steps: **Stop! Look! Listen!**

Whatever you are experiencing now is *not* your past incident.

It's something that is triggering a memory.

Stop! Look! Listen!

I learned this technique originally from bestselling author Arjuna Ardagh, and a variation of what he taught me is the foundation for your fourth Love Spark. These are the steps:

Stop!

Don't think about it, just stop. Stop whatever you are doing, even if you're in the middle of something. Just stop.

Look!

Focus your attention on *one* thing for one minute. One tangible item, like a vase, a tree, a flower, anything, but only one thing.

First, notice the *color* of that thing, and bring all of your attention to its color for fifteen seconds.

Now shift your attention to the *shape* of that one thing for fifteen seconds.

Now shift all of your attention to its *texture* for fifteen seconds.

Finally, including all of it, *focus* on the entirety of that one thing for fifteen seconds.

Listen!

Bring all of your attention to listening now. Listen to your partner, more than with just your ears but with your soul and your spirit. Listen with "all" of you.

When my spouse was very young, he had an experience that left him feeling like he was inadequate and couldn't do anything right. One day, I came home, and he had decorated a wall in our living room. At first glance, I was not satisfied with it. I made comments about things that I would have done differently. I didn't mean this as an attack, but I hit his emotional wound and triggered his feeling of inadequacy.

He became very quiet and serious looking, and I could tell he was hurt.

"Are you alright?" I asked.

It took him a matter of minutes before he said, "No, I'm not. I don't think we can live together anymore."

It was such an extreme statement. I was stunned. My head went into a slight spin. I slowed down and *Stopped! Looked! and Listened!* Once I did that, we were able to move together from the Timeline Life to the Right-Now-Life experience.

Not only was he freed from the pain of my hitting that

emotional wound, but it also brought us closer. We could talk through what was really happening. I told him how proud I was of his willingness to communicate exactly how he felt. And by the way, I love the living room wall now. As it turned out, slowing down gave me a new perspective, too. The distance between us melted like butter on a warm stove.

When you shift to a moment-by-moment experience, you will see more clearly. Slow down. Slow down enough so that you can see your response relates to an *emotional memory* and not to what's actually happening now. When that happens, there's a new beginning for the relationship.

Every heart*ache* and heart*break* leaves a mark. They are defining moments when many parts of your personality were formed. Sharing stories makes you more real to one another and in touch with each other's humanity. Having those moments show up invited, rather than unexpected, makes your relationship stronger and healthier.

When you engage with the heart at an emotional level, having extraordinary events and memories becomes a priority. Memories that add up to a full life. How do we create those exceptional kinds of memories given the day-to-day circumstances of life? Let's take a look.

Fill in the Blanks

Love Spark #1: My Unique Contribution (Giving Away My Deepest Desire): _____

_____

Love Spark #2: My Response to Why (It Is Also My Deepest Desire): _____

_____

Love Spark #3: Letting Go of Judgment

Love Spark #4: Stop! Look! Listen!

Full Moments, on Purpose (Love Spark #5)

When I was in third grade, I brought my lunch to elementary school but had to buy milk in the cafeteria. One day, it tasted funny to me. I smelled it and it smelled funny too, so I didn't drink it.

As I left the cafeteria, there was a nun stationed at the door. Her job was to make sure the students drank their milk. She shook my carton and said, "Go back and drink your milk."

I said, "There's something wrong with it."

She told me there was nothing wrong with it and that if I didn't go back and drink it, she would send me to the principal's office. I had never been in trouble before.

The principal asked me why I would not drink the milk, and I told her. She told me that I was lying and said there was nothing wrong with that milk.

"Tell the truth," she said. And she went on to say that if I didn't tell the truth, she was going to call my father.

That was quite a leap. My father was a public official and for them to bring him into the school was a very big deal. They called in my dad.

"Sister, what seems to be the problem?" Dad said when he arrived.

The principal told him that I didn't want to drink my milk and that I lied about it tasting bad.

My dad looked at me and said, "Son, why won't you drink the milk?"

I said, "Dad, it smells funny, and it tastes bad. I don't wanna drink it."

He looked at the principal and told her he had four other sons.

"If you had told me that any one of them had lied to you, I would have believed it," Dad said. "But this one, he doesn't lie, and he loves milk. Come on son, let's get you home."

My dad knew me and believed me. *That* was a *Full Moment*.

Without a doubt, my mother and father wanted my brothers and me to have very long and very full lives. What most people seem to be focused on, though, is a long life.

I remember hoping to live to be 115 years old. Why? What would I do with it? What would you do with it? Why was a long life considered better than a short one? These questions are what give rise to this Love Spark.

I don't doubt that you wish for your partner, your family, and those that you care for to live very long and full lives. I wonder, though, if you have a clear picture of what that actually means. What is it that you want for yourself? Why do you want it? Can you articulate it?

A long life is simple and means many good quality years. A *Full Life* though is a great life, one full of hope. Maybe there's a little nagging voice in the background that doesn't really think that this is possible. Perhaps you, like most of us, simply settle.

But what good is a long life if it isn't a Full Life? And if that's an appealing inquiry, then we need to articulate what a Full Life is.

A Full Life is a life that is full—full of Full Moments, that's a Full Life. That is a great life. So then, what is a Full Moment?

Full Moments

A Full Moment is not something you imagine. It's not something that you are wishing for or hoping for, and it's not a fantasy or a story.

A Full Moment is something that fills your heart with gratitude, appreciation, and love. I'm trusting that you have had Full Moments that you can look back on. If you take some time and look back on your life, you'll spot some.

Let me share some stories of Full Moments with you.

My brother Ron and I did a Shamanic journey together in the desert areas of San Diego. We drank a little psychoactive cactus juice, and we began to feel the effects. It was the middle of the night, and everyone was wrapped in blankets as we started on a hike. I remember looking over at my brother as we climbed the desert hill and I caught his eye. We both grinned and giggled a little, and in that moment, I felt a deep love and affinity for my brother.

That was a Full Moment.

I interviewed a woman named Jo Anne, and she told me about her close relationship with her mother, who was dying and went into a coma. At one point, her mother opened her eyes.

Jo Anne asked her, "Do you know who I am?"

Her mother replied, "Of course, you're my wonderful daughter, Jo Anne." Then she closed her eyes and passed away.

That was a Full Moment.

I interviewed another woman named Jeanne.

"When I was forty years old, Thomas, I went back to college and got my bachelor's degree. I had not been to school in twenty years," she told me. "I was very excited about it, and I pleaded with my family to come to my graduation, and none of them did. But at the end of the graduation ceremony, I was leaving and saw my stepdad. He was waving at me, making certain that I knew he was there. We had been estranged for years, and yet he showed up for my college graduation!"

That was a Full Moment.

Now for Yours

I now want you to consider some of your Full Moments. Write down anything that you can think of and try to go beyond just the easy ones. One of the characteristics of a Full Moment is that when you think about it or talk about it, you feel the *emotion* of it, you feel the *energy* of it.

Write down some of your Full Moments:

_____

_____

_____

Now look at *who* caused those Full Moments? Did you? Did the people in your life cause them? Most Full Moments happen completely by accident. That doesn't make them any less important, and it doesn't make them any less impactful. But living a Full Life also requires designing Full Moments on purpose.

The Art of Design

I wake up in the morning and I have my routine, just like you. Part of it includes a ritual, one that I invite you to adopt. While you are brushing your teeth, think about your partner and other people whom you love. What are some Full Moments that you could make happen for others, today?

Here are some Full Moments that I made happen. Feel free to use them, and feel free to make them better, then send me an email. I'll use yours too.

I found my partner's favorite song "The Dance" on YouTube. We were getting ready for work when I played the recording. I walked up behind him, gently turned him to face me, and we danced to the song, all the way to the end. We both got emotional, and there wasn't much to say, but the day was off to an amazing start.

That was a Full Moment.

I went through my digital photos and found a special one from years ago. I texted it to my partner with a message: "What do you remember about this moment? I remember …" I added "I love you," and it gave us both the feeling of being connected.

That was a Full Moment.

My partner went to the gym. I snuck over, took his car, and left him mine. I vacuumed and washed it, making it squeaky clean. When I returned it, I left a homemade card on the steering wheel. He was surprised when he got to his shiny car and found my love note. We felt loving and intimate for the rest of the day and into the night.

That was a Full Moment.

On my way home, I saw some lilies on the side of the road. I pulled over and picked one. I snuck in the back door, put the lily on his pillow, then went to the front door and came in as though I had just arrived. When he found the lily, he looked me in the eyes grinning from ear to ear, then hugged me close.

That was a Full Moment.

Notice these are all simple to do, either inexpensive or at no cost at all. **A Full Life is loaded with Full Moments.** Your job is to get good at loading life with these kinds of moments.

It is easy and expected to do this on somebody's birthday, on an anniversary, or on special occasions. Without these occasions, it's not so easy, but it's very effective and extremely rewarding.

Three Elements

There are three things to keep in mind as you create Full Moments: Courage, Letting Go, and Just Say "GO"! Let's consider them, one-by-one:

Courage

- The courage to think beyond spontaneity
- The courage to exercise your creativity
- The courage to expect nothing in return

Why courage, you might wonder? We are trained that spontaneous events, especially where love is involved, are best. This is a romantic notion we learned from TV, movies, books, and songs. It's not true. Planning and executing within the real circumstances of your relationship is much more romantic and real. This expresses *true love*.

It is not easy to be creative (for some, it is downright difficult), so it requires courage to step into that possible discomfort. Lastly, there is no guarantee that your partner will love everything you do. They may express gratitude and make you feel happy or they might remain neutral.

Letting Go

- Letting Go of resistance
- Letting Go of resentment
- Letting Go of regret

You and I do not wake up every morning "feeling the love." Heck, we don't wake up every morning even loving ourselves. Letting go is necessary to have and create full lives and good relationships. You might resist doing something "sweet or nice." You might have resentment for something that just happened or didn't happen. You might regret how you have been. All of these require Letting Go.

Just say "GO"!

Courage and Letting Go allow you to be more vulnerable. You might not like feeling vulnerable. You may want to STOP when you feel vulnerable. I want you to just say GO. A great life, a Full Life, is a championship game, and a champion says GO when others say STOP.

These elements are about more than trying to make somebody feel good or even make somebody happy. These are ways for you to ignite the human spirit. Igniting the human spirit ignites your relationships. You are contributing to creating great lives, full lives, on purpose.

The Fifth Love Spark is Full Moments, on Purpose.

Full Moments by accident are powerful, but the ones you cause on purpose are true gifts from the heart. You are using your energy to make them special and to make them happen.

What's really cool is you can't cause a Full Moment for someone else on purpose without experiencing it yourself. In fact, many times I experience that feeling as I am writing them on my list. I haven't even done them yet! This will probably happen for you, too. It's the best LOVE magic on the planet!

The practice of this Love Spark naturally gives you a new appetite, one that is hungry for speaking the *Language of Love*. What is the Language of Love? How do you speak it, and how do you understand it? Follow me, we'll get into that next.

Fill in the Blanks

Love Spark #1: My Unique Contribution (Giving Away My Deepest Desire): _____

_____

Love Spark #2: My Response to Why (It Is Also My Deepest Desire): _____

_____

Love Spark #3: Letting Go of Judgment

Love Spark #4: Stop! Look! Listen!

Love Spark #5: Full Moments, on Purpose

For-Giveness (Love Spark #6)

> "To let go does not mean to get rid of. To let go means to let be. When we let be with compassion, things come and go on their own."
>
> —**Jack Kornfield,** author and Buddhist practitioner

I often think how important my relationship is to me and how important romantic love is to so many people. After all, isn't that why you are reading this book?

I don't think a single one of us has said to ourselves, "I hope one day that I have a somewhat interesting, average, and ordinary relationship. I hope we don't fight very often, and I hope that we connect sometimes, perhaps even having sex once in a while!"

Nobody ever says that! Most of us have greater hopes regarding our intimate relationships. We want relationships that stand out.

We want to know that we are loved and cherished above anyone else. We want to have constructive conversations together that make a difference. And we want love-making that is intimate and **on** fire. And yet, Bad Relationship Habits leave many couples wanting more.

Challenges in our relationships and in our everyday lives are unavoidable.

The Love Spark that will help you to embrace the realities of life and deal with life's ups and downs is the Language of Love. This is an unconventional approach that makes possible the experience of love, even in the face of everything that comes your way.

Developing the Language of Love

The Language of Love is FORGIVENESS.

Now, have an open mind. I know you have an understanding of forgiveness. You're probably very good at it or, at least, you try to be. Let's look at forgiveness in a deeper way by breaking it down.

The first part of forgiveness is "for," as in you are for something. As a sports fan is for their team. You are "for"-giving. Not giving as in gifting, but rather, giving as in "to allow for."

Allowing or making room for your partner is the Language of Love. Accessing this language begins with *letting go* of your automatic reactions to your partner not being how you think they should be.

Instead, allow for the way they *are*. That's for-giving. Let go of your kneejerk responses and stop finding reasons to be upset. Letting go gives you access to this kind of forgiveness.

For-giving also eliminates judgment: the judgment of yourself, your past, your flaws, your failures, and even your accomplishments.

Judgment robs you of the experience of love. Forgiveness, on the other hand, allows for the experience, the expression, and the expansion of love, no matter what.

No matter what!

Forgiveness *allows* for problems, troubles, and insecurities. It takes into account that they will happen. It allows for another's humanity and your own.

It is this kind of forgiveness that, after a major challenge, allows a couple to be *whole* again. It determines their future. Each day and every moment, you and I decide how we will respond in the face of what's happening, whatever the circumstance. You can give power to your reaction or you can give power to the practice of letting go. From there, you can recreate your relationship.

Long-lasting, happy couples have this in common: They are *for*-giving, and they practice the Language of Love. It is both a practice and a habit to be developed. Wanting to be married or coupled, wanting to thrive, gives fuel to this practice.

Apologizing: The Plan

There is another way that we deal with forgiveness. Saying "I'm sorry" is the most common and rather ordinary way. Every relationship includes apologies. We all make mistakes. Many times, one needs to be sorry while the other needs to be able to receive it. This restores the experience of love.

More often than we like to admit, saying I'm sorry can actually be a way of saying "Now, get off my back." If that's where you are, then move past that attitude and consider what you really want.

Do you want the experience of love? Do you want peace and harmony? Are you past playing games? If so, then take the time to plan what you will say the next time you find yourself in hot water.

Apologizing needs to include *what happened* so that both of you are talking about the same thing in the same way. It needs to include *admitting the hurt or upset* you may have caused. That will ease some of the tension.

With less tension, saying *I'm sorry* can begin a natural conversation for your partner to express how they feel. Hearing how they feel, then *asking for forgiveness*, leads to what's needed to *restore the relationship*.

This is the hardest part. Sometimes, no matter what you say or do, it isn't enough. This includes apologies to anyone. Sometimes people may hesitate to forgive because they need something from you or just need more time. Or perhaps you are someone whose apologies have become so commonplace as to be meaningless. You've used them loosely and so often that your partner can't even hear you.

Ask them what you can do to make this right. This shows that you are willing to do whatever it takes. You may not understand their emotions, but it is important to allow for their experience.

Accepting an apology isn't always easy, either. Sometimes it's the depth of the trespass that gets in the way. We all have a line and perhaps that line has been crossed. Maybe your partner has made the same offenses, again and again, so it feels like a throwaway line when they say I'm sorry.

It's a big deal. And if you are going to stay in the relationship, you must manage your feelings and opinions. The goal is to get to a place where you can *authentically* accept apologies.

Here's How

Listen to the apology with "all" of you, not just your ears but with your heart and your soul. Then, *be honest* about what you will need. If you need more time, ask for it.

You might not get everything you ask for, but the conversation can begin. **To forgive is to close the gap and become one again.**

An apology, when needed, cannot be replaced with anything else, or can it? Instead of avoiding and saying nothing, try replacing that I'm sorry with two different words: *Thank you*. Not an off-handed kind of thank you, but one that could change a mistake into a learning moment. Thanking your partner for working through something yet again, instead of saying "I'm sorry," might land much better. It could open up a new conversation that makes a difference.

Naturally, you will need to test this out yourself, which is exactly what I expect you to do. It will take some thought as you start because there will be times when a regular "I'm sorry" will seem to be the only choice. Try "thank you" a few times, and you will see where it can be a favorable option. When I practice it, I find that it takes some consideration as to how the "thank you" might work.

One day, I was walking through the house to get to the kitchen, deep in thought. I passed my spouse along the way, and he asked me a detailed question. I just didn't have the mental space for his question at the time and I was sharp-tongued as I told him, "I can't deal with this right now."

Argh! I realized right in that very moment that I had slipped into my Bad Relationship Habit. Never having time to do it right, but always having time to do it over, I went back to him and got his attention.

I said, "Thank you. Thank you for not having a reaction to my attitude. Can I do that over?" And I did!

You can see in this instance, "I'm sorry" would be the usual response and might have got the job done. Saying "thank you," though, gave us a different kind of do-over. The remorse and bad feelings went away immediately.

Swapping out these words is a small change to make. It will take some more effort at first but will be worth it for the amazing impact. Sometimes, you might have noticed feeling guilty when you say "I'm sorry" so often. It can cast a dark shadow over the conversation—like starting things off on the wrong foot. Switching that negative "I'm sorry" to a positive "thank you" can move you more quickly to recovery. You will spend less time mentally obsessing over your screwup and create a natural segue to being together with ease.

I have found this approach handles more than half of the apologies I deliver. As an example, I accidentally knocked over a good friend's favorite vase. It went crashing to the floor. I hardly think *thank you* would have been appropriate. The better response was "I'm sorry, let's get you a new vase."

If you put this practice into action, you will find your communications improve. It will transform uncomfortable exchanges into something constructive and upbeat.

What more could you want?

How about a reduction in the need for an ordinary kind of forgiveness? This Love Spark, the Language of Love, is the *most powerful* kind of *for*-giving and is accessible by using the practice of Letting Go.

This Love Spark is to be For-Giving. I call it The Language of Love.

Relationships are not necessarily easy, but they are extremely rewarding. We have covered so much. Is there anything else you can do to make an *even bigger* difference in your relationship?

Something simple and extremely easy to learn? In fact, there is, and we'll explore that next.

Fill in the Blanks

Love Spark #1: My Unique Contribution (Giving Away My Deepest Desire): _____

_____

Love Spark #2: My Response to Why (It Is Also My Deepest Desire): _____

_____

Love Spark #3: Letting Go of Judgment

Love Spark #4: Stop! Look! Listen!

Love Spark #5: Full Moments, on Purpose

Love Spark #6: For-Giveness, the Language of Love

Sliding Door Moments (Love Spark #7)

> "I'm not upset that you lied to me.
> I'm upset that from now on, I can't believe you."
>
> —**Friedrich Nietzsche,** philosopher

The telephone rang, and it was Michael, a friend of my boyfriend at the time.

"Hi Michael," I said. "Bruce isn't here. He's in Bowling Green visiting his family."

"I know," he said, "I'm not calling for Bruce. I called to talk with you."

"OK," I said, "What's up?"

It was no secret I had never been very fond of Michael. He made it evident that he had a crush on my boyfriend, even though he is the one who introduced us. I always managed to keep a little distance from him and avoided his company. Bruce liked him, though, and they would often hang out.

On this call, Michael was trying to come off as my friend. He proceeded to ask me if I knew what Bruce was up to every weekend when visiting "back home"?

"Up to?" I proclaimed, "He's visiting his mom and dad."

"You need to ask him," he told me. "You are very trusting, and he is playing you."

I thanked him and ended the conversation, not for a moment believing anything he told me that was going on with Bruce. Bruce and I talked every night while he was away, and I was quite comfortable in the relationship. Trust was not an issue.

I told Bruce about the call I had with Michael and he shrugged it off, saying, "You know how Michael is. He's just jealous."

And that is what I believed.

Three weeks later, I got a phone call from a girl in Bowling Green.

She said, "Hi, I'm Tracy, Bruce's fiancée. We have an engagement party planned next weekend, and I wanted to invite Bruce's friends from Louisville as a surprise. Can you come?"

I was surprised all right!

Romantic love is a risky business. It's an act of faith, and it's the price you pay for admission.

The trust ticket gets you the love ride, which is exciting partly because it's full of surprises. The surprises are a mixture of good and bad and can make some people fearful. If you are one of those fearful people, then you might find trusting difficult. But even though it's difficult, it is possible.

Opening and Closing

While trust opens your heart to grow and expand, broken trust can close your heart. Closing your heart might feel safer, but it robs you of fully experiencing life.

An open heart allows for the experience of caring, goodwill, and empathy. This gives rise to other emotions like safety, connectedness, and feeling cared for. These euphoric emotions drive our relationships.

To trust means to be carefree or free from concern. It means to have confidence and to be able to rely on the integrity, fairness, honesty, and friendship of another person. As you look at trust in your relationship, you want to be able to know what you can count on from your partner.

The Pathway to Trust

Many couples tell me how they need to rebuild or restore trust in their relationships. Trust cannot be restored in and of itself. **Trust is the endgame**.

What is the pathway to trust? Any pathway has to have something definable and measurable to keep you on that path, so you know where to focus your attention. When it comes to trust, *trustworthiness* is what's measurable and definable.

To be trustworthy, however, is merely to be *worthy* of trust, and this is where the plot thickens. There needs to be an understanding for giving and expecting trust. A basis or foundation that consists of actions and attitudes that express in which ways you and your partner are trustworthy. One only needs to watch the actions of another to determine how they can be trusted. Everyone can be trusted for something, even if they are only trusted "not" to do something.

I've found that there are three key elements to trustworthiness.

If you develop your trustworthiness in the eyes of your partner, and they do for you, then that is a basis for building more trust. There needs to be evidence you are both *trustworthy*, and generating this evidence can be one of the richest opportunities of being in love.

For example, my spouse is extremely loyal. I know I can trust him in any area where loyalty is involved. However, I cannot trust him to be on time or with anything that requires a lot of detail. When we had this conversation together, he agreed to work on this as a way to increase his trustworthiness. It has been an incredible gift because now, more often than not, I can trust him to be on time.

He tells me that he can trust me in almost all areas. Where he cannot trust me is when I disappear into my home office, leaving him without a clue as to when he might see me again. This is frustrating for him and diminishes trust. He wants to know when he can count on my being with him. Now, I cook every day at 5:00 p.m., serve dinner by 6:00 p.m., and then we spend the rest of the evening together.

This raises our level of intimacy and expands our experience of love.

The Two of You

Now it's your turn. Where is your opportunity to build trustworthiness? I organized "lists of trust areas," one for each of the three elements that follow. I suggest you and your partner go through them together to determine both of your expectations when it comes to trustworthiness. Feel free to add to these lists so the two of you can have some productive conversations.

In what areas are we each *capable*?

- Managing children
- Setting up travel or parties
- Cooking dinner or grocery shopping
- Coordinating our schedules
- Opening up about difficult topics
- Accepting responsibility for mistakes
- Paying the bills
- Being on time

_____

_____

_____

In what areas are we each less than completely *honest*? (And where do we each draw the line?)

- Income taxes
- Faking a headache to get out of something
- Harboring secrets
- Telling the truth
- Gossiping or complaining about others
- Covering up mistakes
- Spending

_____

_____

_____

In what ways are we each *reliable*?

- Showing up on time
- Doing what we say
- Remembering birthdays, anniversaries, and essential dates
- Honoring things that matter
- Keeping secrets in confidence
- Paying the bills
- Picking up the kids from school
- Treating in-laws and family with respect

_____

_____

_____

Getting on the same page with your partner and measuring yourselves against the same principles will strengthen your bond.

When it comes to capabilities and honesty, my spouse is strong. Reliability is an area where he has some room to grow, but this is an acceptable compromise for me. Where I can trust him *far outweighs* the areas where I cannot.

Remember your Conditions of Satisfaction from Chapter Three? As long as the top conditions are met most of the time, having the others met some of the time is an easy compromise.

The Truth

Trusting makes the world a more open, inviting, and friendly place. It has no guarantees, but studies show that to be completely happy, we need it.

Trust is the one thing that changes everything.

Studies reveal that those who are trusting are happier. They are more accepted by others, and they tend to be more honest. The degree to which we can trust others correlates with the level of contentment we experience.

Though it might be fair to say that we all value honesty and want to be honest, we sometimes value other qualities more—qualities such as loyalty, kindness, and sensitivity. When these are at odds with the truth, you might resort to an innocent lie—defined here as dishonesty for another person's sake.

Even if someone lies to you for your own good, you may struggle to feel all right about it. It disrupts your belief that you are on a level playing field, and studies show that a level playing field is universally important to all of us. When you lie, you could be putting up a wall between you and the person to whom you are lying.

When you think of lying to someone you care about, it's important to consider: Who does this lie protect? Does it protect your partner or is it protecting you?

Lying, when habitual, is a slippery slope. Even justifiable lies can make a liar unable to be vulnerable in the relationship.

Can a couple have a great relationship even if they lie to other people once in a while? Studies indicate yes, provided the couple maintains a higher standard with one another.

A good place to begin building trust with your partner is to determine your moral code as a couple and where you draw the line.

That higher standard is a Couple's Code of Honor, and trust is part of that unique moral code. Later on, you and your partner will have an opportunity to work on your Couple's Code of Honor.

When Your Partner Breaks Your Trust

Betrayals, big and small, can take a toll on our ability to trust our partners and result in our shutting down and closing our hearts. The greatest deception is infidelity. There are others, but that is the biggest.

Consider these stories of betrayal:

Adrienne spent eighteen years with her significant other, only to find he was having an ongoing affair. She was heartbroken, angry, felt betrayed, and embarassed. Of course, she needed time to grieve. After a while, she became more willing to look closely at herself and her role in the relationship. What she found amazed her. She realized that she was always "looking for the next one." This had never occurred to her before. Her betrayal was that she was not 100 percent invested in the relationship. This was an eye-opener for her, so much so that she was able to apologize to her spouse and let him go. They remain friends.

Robert came home unexpectedly and found his spouse of fifteen years, along with his business partner, naked and wrapped in towels. They had obviously just stepped out of the shower together. He was dumbfounded, hurt, and confused. Robert had to confront that things had gone wrong right under his nose. He questioned every moment in the relationship, and the burden was unbearable. He felt that he had been clueless and never saw it coming. They decided to figure out together what had led to this outcome and took the time to discuss it as a couple. The cheating spouse said that she had never felt like the top priority in Robert's world. Career and other hobbies took first place. She wanted him, but she did not sign up to play second. Robert took responsibility for putting his career first. He also acknowledged that that would likely never change, and they decided to separate.

Daniel was met at the door by his spouse Angela in tears. She told him she had been having an affair for two years, and it had just been broken off. She wanted to come clean because the strain was unbearable for her, and she was suffering the loss of the affair. She was disoriented but still loved Daniel and wanted to work it out. Angela was willing to work on the marriage and take responsibility for the betrayal. It was not easy for either of them, but after a series of coaching sessions, they built new trust, putting the relationship first, and they recently celebrated their twenty-fifth anniversary.

Some of the common thoughts that people have after finding out their partners had been unfaithful are: "What an idiot I am, what an idiot! And then every red flag started to flash across my mind." "Oh my gosh, what is wrong with me? How did I miss this? ARGH!!!" "My whole life feels like it is caved in." "I can barely stand, my stomach is tight, and I am literally screaming." "I can no longer trust. The gamble is too great, and the pain of defeat too intense. I am jaded."

We often think of trust as associated with the big things, but most betrayals are subtle and happen during daily interactions that psychological researcher Dr. John Gottman, of The Gottman Institute, calls "Sliding Door Moments."

My spouse Rafael and I have an agreement. Because I work with clients on Zoom, he does not walk in without checking first to see if I am busy. Instead, he will peek his head in the door first. It's rare that he even does that. One day, I was on Zoom, though not with a client, and I was about to let him walk away.

Instead, I called out, "Rafael, come in, I am talking with Melodye, say hello."

He smiled and walked back in and said, "Hello."

That was a Sliding Door Moment. Calling him back into the office acknowledged his importance to me. Having your important people feel important when they are with you is a trust-builder.

Have you ever missed an elevator? How about just making one? That is how you want to think of a Sliding Door Moment. It's an opportunity that you can choose to miss or not. I could have easily let Rafael walk back into the house, and it would not have been a problem. But the instant I considered calling him back, that was the Sliding Door Moment. When you catch them, they build trust in your relationship.

By giving your partner a particular kind of generosity or thoughtfulness, you remind them why they are with you and that they are important to you.

Take Advantage of Sliding Door Moments

You know you *should* pay more attention. You know you *should* catch every Sliding Door Moment. But "shoulds" never get you what you really want. Are you curious as to what you might do with all those "shoulds" that you carry around? What if those "shoulds" are your gateway to having exactly what you want?

Fill in the Blanks

Love Spark #1: My Unique Contribution (Giving Away My Deepest Desire): _____

_____

Love Spark #2: My Response to Why (It Is Also My Deepest Desire): _____

_____

Love Spark #3: Letting Go of Judgment

Love Spark #4: Stop! Look! Listen!

Love Spark #5: Full Moments, on Purpose

Love Spark #6: For-Giveness, the Language of Love

Love Spark #7: Take Advantage of Sliding Door Moments

The Couple's Code of Honor

> "Anyone who achieves something magnificent in
> their life turns their 'shoulds' into 'musts.'"
>
> **—Tony Robbins,** bestselling author and motivational speaker

It was a sunny day in Northern California, and I was out with my spouse enjoying a hike at Pacific Beach. We had discussed coming back the next night for sunset and then headed home. While in the car, I was deep in thought about some last-minute work I need to catch up on so I could be 100 percent with him at home. While I was thinking, he asked me to search for the time for tomorrow night's sunset, not a big request, right? Right!

I thought to myself, I'm busy. Why is he asking me to do this? Why can't he do it?

Out loud, I replied, with some attitude, "You can do that, can't you?"

He responded, "OK, fine. I'll do it when I get home."

I could tell from the tone in his voice that he was not pleased. Not angry, but definitely not happy. I felt his energy shift, and I certainly didn't want that.

"You know, I never do that to you. Never," he said. "When you need something or ask anything of me, I never act like you are a bother, and you always do that to me. Acting that way makes me feel like what I do doesn't measure up. It makes me feel like I don't do anything of value and that I am insignificant. After all, you are the technical guy, and I am the domestic one."

Damn. He was right.

First, I always do that. I react like he is a bother. His point is valid.

Second, he *never* does that. This is actually one of those times that when he says *never*, it really is *never*.

And third, I do believe that I have more going on than he does. His request felt like an interruption. Our day-to-day lives are entirely different, and I believe that he has no grasp on how I plan every minute.

Ouch! Did I just miss a Sliding Door Moment?

Yes, I did. The Sliding Door Moment was the moment I copped an attitude. I could have used that moment to build trust in our relationship by dropping the attitude and simply making an authentic request. I didn't even need to do what he asked me to do. I just needed to respond like what he wanted mattered.

As you can see, you will sometimes miss the mark just like I did, and that does not mean complete failure. It's a missed opportunity but not a lost cause.

"Shoulds"

I really *should* change my attitude. I really, really *should*! Don't you agree?

I *should* be a better husband. I *should* appreciate, in a significant way, everything he does for us. I am not alone in this kind of internal dialogue. I am confident you can relate to what I am saying.

How often do you think:

- I should be more appreciative.
- I should be more understanding.
- I should be more patient.
- I should do my part without complaint.
- I should be the one that always leaves my spouse feeling good.

While a "should" can exist in any area of your life, let's focus on your relationship. Most people have an endless list of things they believe they *should* do. And these carry about the same weight as a typical New Year's resolution. If it happens, then that's great. If not, you won't be too disappointed because you knew it wasn't going to happen anyway.

Where you find yourself saying "should," I encourage you to investigate. When does this happen? What kinds of things do your "shoulds" involve?

Take a moment and write some down:

_____
_____
_____

"Musts"

What happens when you decide something is an absolute must? The mind cuts off any option except to succeed. The idea behind turning "shoulds" into "musts" is that it means you don't settle for less. Making the decision that you will find a way to make something happen raises your standard, and higher standards impact your relationship dramatically.

Test your "shoulds" by turning them into "must" statements. If the "must" statement rings true for you, then you know it is an area where raising your standards will be important.

Here are some of mine:

- I must change my attitude.
- I must be a better husband.
- I must appreciate, in a significant way, everything he does for us.

Now, turn your "shoulds" into "musts":

_____

_____

_____

Raising Your Standards

Your relationship is a direct reflection of the standards you hold. For example, some people are in a relationship, and they aren't happy. Their standard may be "I must be in a relationship." This standard is too low because it allows for any kind of relationship.

What if they *raise* their standard to "I must have a passionate and loving connection"? That standard can be met in *any* relationship, not just an intimate one.

Others may not be in a relationship because their standard is "I must avoid heart*ache* or heart*break*" or "I must not be hurt," and that standard does not allow for an intimate relationship.

Now is the time to raise the bar and turn your "shoulds" into "musts." That's how you redefine yourself and your relationship. For now, identify one or two standards you are ready to work with, and write them down.

For example:

- I only accept people who act the way I like.
- People take advantage of me.
- I do not feel emotionally supported.
- I do not like to argue and fight in my relationship.

_____

_____

_____

Now, turn them into "should" statements. For example:

- I should be more accepting.
- I should not be taken advantage of.
- I should feel emotionally supported.
- We should get along with each other.

_____

_____

_____

Next, turn them into "must" sentences. For example:

- I must accept myself and others as they are.
- I must give voice to my boundaries.
- I must be responsible for my emotional well-being.
- We must honor and respect one another's views.

_____

_____

_____

When you expect more from yourself, you won't have to voice what you expect from your partner. They will either be able to reciprocate your wishes, or they won't. Standards start within, and what you have written are your new standards.

Now, decide with 100 percent conviction that you will honor them.

Stay true to your new standards, and you are on your way to **A Relationship on Fire**!

Couple's Code of Honor

Raising the standards in your relationship will have you looking for ways to help maintain them. A Code of Honor is a perfect way to do that. It opens a lot of opportunities for communicating between you and your partner. This process is not limited to couples; everyone can use a Code of Honor in their lives. A Code of Honor starts with you.

Before you start out on this quest, it is essential to answer these two questions:

What is your Deepest Desire?

What Do You Stand For?

You know your Deepest Desire, so now it's time to determine What You Stand For. When two people embark on the journey of being a couple; it is a journey of discovery, of exploring your souls and your purpose together.

Consciously creating your partnership demands that these questions be answered. Couples who are aware of what they want and why they want it will manage to get it. They are united in what they stand for.

Whether you realize it or not, you are on a journey that will include many unknowns. You will encounter a variety of situations, and standards will help support you in your decisions. The Couple's Code of Honor is that kind of standard. It is a set of agreements that you and your partner decide to stand for during your life together. These agreements need to be strong and simple; they do not need to be complicated. They can be changed, as needed, as your desires as a couple evolve and grow.

Both of you have been raised with a particular set of ethical and moral principles. You may have been taught these by your family, culture, society, and even religion. You carry these into your relationship. You will now create with your partner your own personal Couple's Code of Honor. This is a living document that may take several versions until the two of you are satisfied. Enjoy the process.

By way of example, I have included my Couple's Code of Honor next. It is simple, making it very easy to follow. We laminated and placed it so it is always visible in our bedroom near our Rules of Engagement (Chapter Ten). This supports us through difficult conversations when we need to have them.

Our Couple's Code of Honor

We love unconditionally. Unconditional love is an ongoing practice in any relationship. It is expressed and experienced by letting go of our opinions and allowing one another and all people to be who they are. It is never a consideration about whether we like the traits, characteristics, style, personality, or beliefs of those individuals. It does not mean we agree with them; it just means we can let them be who they are and love them as they are.

We choose to be close. We will share our closeness with others, being generous while maintaining a consistent amount of closeness with one another. We will never desert each other or our children when in need, danger, or trouble. We will never permit our affinity to be contaminated.

We respect each other's energy. We will share our time, money, and resources as we are able.

We are forgiving. If we should fail in our efforts to act in ways that are consistent with our Couple's Code of Honor, we will ask for forgiveness as soon as we are aware, and we agree to be forgiving. We also commit to being forgiving of others and to never hold a grudge, realizing that to hold on to anything negative will ultimately affect our relationship together.

We share our experiences. We will share our dreams, visions, and what we learn with each other and others as openly as we think will make a difference. We will never undervalue ourselves, one another, or minimize the strength of us as a couple.

We find contentment with yesterday's events. Life is happening now, and we will make every effort to live into a brighter future. We will let go of past failures, upsets, and difficulties. We let go of any regrets immediately.

We live in harmony and balance with nature. We agree that the planet and all of its inhabitants need to be protected and that our interactions matter.

We live life fully. We will make our decisions and choices based on what matters most to us, individually and as a couple. We value invitations, and we will engage with others because we choose to, not because we should.

Here are some other ideas you may want to consider for your Couple's Code of Honor:

- We will obey the laws of the land.
- We will seek the divine in all things.
- We put God first.
- We agree to honor the Rules of Engagement. (Next chapter)
- We are dedicated to wisdom, and a desire to learn, grow, and deepen our understanding of people and the world around us.
- We will be courageous, doing the right thing even when it might cost us.
- We will take a leap, even when the prospects are scary.
- We agree to live debt-free.
- We agree to make travel a priority.
- We agree to keep a tidy and clean home.
- We will hold honesty as the foundation of our union.
- We will respect and honor one another.

Your Couple's Code of Honor will be the one thing you can depend on throughout your life together. Not every possible option is listed here, and there is nothing off limits if you agree to it. The code is created from your hearts and souls and can be counted on to continually keep your standards high. No one is perfect, and every couple fails to keep the Couple's Code of Honor on occasion.

In fact, there will be times in a healthy, loving relationship where you will argue for your point of view. But if you argue, then it's good to have some Rules of Engagement, don't you agree?

Fill in the Blanks

Love Spark #1: My Unique Contribution (Giving Away My Deepest Desire): _____

_____

Love Spark #2: My Response to Why (It Is Also My Deepest Desire): _____

_____

Love Spark #3: Letting Go of Judgment

Love Spark #4: Stop! Look! Listen!

Love Spark #5: Full Moments, on Purpose

Love Spark #6: For-Giveness, the Language of Love

Love Spark #7: Take Advantage of Sliding Door Moments

Tools

Code of Honor

Rules of Engagement

In 1985, Rafael built his dream home, where we now live together, and each room has an artistic flair. The design of our kitchen, however, is not straightforward. It's very artistic, and it doesn't have day-to-day cooking as the top priority.

Though this makes for a beautiful and interesting presentation, the kitchen is not always functional. I've occasionally made comments about the kitchen design because I am the one who does most of the shopping and cooking, and I find it frustrating.

On this particular day, I was standing in the kitchen preparing a meal, and the layout was more irritating than usual. Making our dinner is my pleasure, but the setup can be extremely awkward: pots and pans separated (I find some in the garage, some under the sink, and some next to the oven), mixing bowls on the other side of the room. You get the idea. Trying to get things done, and not finding the things I need near where they are needed, can be very frustrating.

"My gosh," I exclaimed. "Can we not have anything workable?

Does everything have to be a major chore around here? I just don't understand it."

I wanted or needed to express my exasperation out loud.

When I turned around, my spouse was gone. I didn't think much of it until I saw my text. It was from him, and it read, "Thomas, I had to leave and I will be gone for a while. Please don't try calling me or texting me, I am turning off my phone. I don't want to talk to you right now."

I was confused and anxious. I didn't know what made him leave, but I honored his request and didn't try to reach him.

He returned more than three hours later. He seemed to be himself so I asked him, "Do you want to talk about what happened?"

He looked at me puzzled and said, "You don't know?"

"No," I said, "I'm not sure. Did it have to do with what I said about the kitchen?"

He nodded and continued, "I just can't seem to make you happy. We have a beautiful home that many people would love to live in. The kitchen is my masterpiece, it is my art. And you don't appreciate my art."

I had on several occasions tried to make changes to it after I became our main cook. The requests I made were reasonable and doable from my point of view, but every time I mentioned it, I only hit a wall with him. He would argue until I felt beaten down, and I would give up.

It would go something like this, "Thomas, all you have to do is walk over there and back, it's only fifteen seconds."

I responded by saying, "Yes, that is true, but my hands are wet or they are engaged in the food prep and I need what I need right here, in the area where the cooking is actually happening."

I just couldn't win, so I would give up. Well, sort of.

As I listened to him this time, I realized we were having an argument and not a debate. It started with my flippant remarks about our kitchen, knowing full well that it was his design and that he was sensitive about it. I could say that I didn't intentionally hurt his feelings, but that is a pretense. I really didn't want to have a full-blown argument, but I did want to make my point, and I did it in a passive-aggressive way.

Have you ever found an argument sneak up on you and your partner? An interruption that seemed like it came out of nowhere? Something that had been lingering, and you knew it was lingering, but never dealt with it? That's what happened to us that day.

The buildup of frustration led to my flippant remarks. For him, it felt like a hit below the belt and he was hurt. Leaving before he said something that he might regret seemed his safest option.

This was not workable, and something had to change. That is what led us to develop our Rules of Engagement.

Avoiding Landmines

Do you ever feel like you are having the same fight over and over, knowing it won't ever get resolved? Do you sometimes resort to passive-aggressive behavior trying to be heard without actually doing anything about it? Are there instances where an old argument starts up again when you are in the middle of something else—on your way to a dinner party or headed out the door to go to work?

All couples have a way that they fight or disagree. You and your partner have boundaries, some are spoken and some are not. In my story, I found an unspoken boundary: Our home is personal to him. It represents his art. I learned that this had to be handled with care.

After that discovery, we were able to get to the bottom of things and came up with a plan to redesign the kitchen. It now meets my needs while at the same time honoring and appreciating his artistic flair. We both win.

Another unspoken boundary involves the fact that I sometimes cuss when I'm angry. But I have learned that if I do that when we argue, he will shut down and push me away. Now, I don't use foul language when we disagree. One boundary that he learned about me is that he cannot just walk away. He has to express himself, even if he only tells me he wants more time to think it through. Disappearing or shutting down doesn't work for me. So he doesn't do that anymore, he speaks up.

What are your boundaries? What are your partner's boundaries? How pushy or loud do you think you need to be for your partner to get your point? Are there things that you do or say that push your partner away?

When you push to be heard, you can step on landmines you didn't even know were there. Bumping into unknown boundaries (landmines) can take you off track and into a brand-new fight.

Can You Remain Close?

With a clear set of rules, you will stay on track, taking the luck out of getting to a resolution. The development of these rules will bring up conversations that matter to you both. These will be your Rules of Engagement. Having something spoken and agreed upon has power. Spending some time talking about your boundaries and expectations will keep you close even when you disagree.

How boring would it be if we were always like-minded? Our emotions run high when we discuss the things that matter *most* with the person who matters *most*. A significant part of our free time is spent with this one person, this wonderful, loving, and sometimes infuriating person.

Over time, partners who are in a healthy relationship will instinctively develop *friendly fighting* skills. They grow to understand that friction is a natural occurrence for couples.

Friendly fighting means to share things you are passionate about with passion. It includes blowing off steam without burning or getting burnt. It does not include name-calling or personal attacks. How you disagree and argue needs ground rules. If you have rules and follow them, you will have established, agreed-upon ways to make your points.

Hitting below the belt can sometimes feel like the only way to get your point across, but at a very high cost. My being flippant with Rafael and his walking out could have led down a dark and lonely road. The Rules of Engagement, which vary from couple to couple, are a handy tool, especially in difficult times.

Rules of Engagement

Let's take a look at some of the rules that could work for your relationship. It helps to have a starting point when developing these rules more formally, and that would be the points you already agree upon.

By the way, don't involve family or friends in this discussion. It's unfair to your partner and can diminish trust. Everybody has an opinion, and the cost of those opinions can be damaging.

The best way I can introduce you to actual rules is to share ours. We have them laminated next to our Couple's Code of Honor in our bedroom. They are:

Rule #1: Set Aside Time with Ideal Conditions for the Discussion (Fight)

We allow time to process a bit before we talk. Matters that are important enough to argue about are important enough to set the right time and place to discuss. And there is no need for a marathon. Set the pace that works for you (see Rule #9).

Rule #2: Fighting in Front of Others

Fighting in front of your kids or other people can be a particularly toxic behavior. If something happens to break out when we are with others, we step away or agree to wait until we're alone.

Rule #3: Describe Your Feelings—Don't Become Them

"I feel" or "it seems like" is the best way to start an awkward conversation, such as:

I *feel* angry versus *physically hitting something*
I *feel* furious versus *actually yelling and screaming*
I *feel* sad or I *feel* hurt versus *shutting down*
It *seems* like you are angry versus *what are you mad about?*
It *seems* like you want to be alone versus *why don't you want to be with me?*
It *seems* like you don't appreciate me versus *quit attacking me.*

Rule# 4: Stay Away from Absolutes (Never, Always, Every)

Absolutes make one of you synonymous with the problem. It might feel like a personal attack. For example, when you start with "you always," "you never," "how could you," it can put one of you on the defensive and diminish your ability to reach a resolution.

Rule #5: Listen

No one wants to hear that they "shouldn't" *feel* a particular way. Respectful listening includes not interrupting one another, taking the time to reflect back what you understood, and being focused on the feelings behind one other's words.

Rule #6: Choose Your Words Wisely

Slow down. Take the time to use the words that you really mean. In a heated discussion, it is easy to say things you might not be able to take back.

Rule #7: Talk in a Reasonable Tone

Using a sharp tone or yelling rarely gets your point across, and it does not necessarily make one heard. Even if one of you yells, there's no need to yell back. Keep the volume down. Also, no hitting or name-calling.

Rule #8: Don't Attack Each Other's Character

You know each other's weaknesses and vulnerabilities, so don't go there. Making a point doesn't need to inflict pain, and nobody needs to be made out to be a villain.

Rule #9: Set a Time Limit

Forty-five minutes is a good amount of time to talk. If you need longer, then take a break every thirty minutes or so. If the two of you are people who need a few hours, plan it.

Rule #10: Read the Other Person's Body Language

Your partner is always communicating something, and that communication includes words as well as tone of voice, facial expressions, and body language.

You and your partner can pick and choose rules that make the most sense for your relationship. Start here. (You can always refine them until you are both satisfied.)

Rule #1: _____

Rule #2: _____

Rule #3: _____

Rule #4: _____

Rule #5: _____

Rule #6: _____

Rule #7: _____

Rule #8: _____

Rule #9: _____

Rule #10: _____

Finding Common Ground

Here are some tips for a constructive argument:

- There are likely some points of agreement, and that's where to start.
- Identify and deal with the issue at hand; avoid getting sidetracked.
- Don't ignore anything relevant to this one issue, and be open to a quick resolution.
- Invite collaboration, offer alternatives, and remain open.
- Recognize that the two of you have different realities that are merely clashing.
- Fighting is no time for mind-reading or interpretation.
- Watch out for the tendency to shame, blame, or attack.
- Validation is not agreeing; it is acknowledging your partner has a point.
- Fighting ends when cooperation begins.

Make Repair Attempts as You Go

Repair attempts de-escalate an argument, and either of you can put on the brakes. These attempts keep a disagreement from spinning out of control. It's essential to get good at repair attempts. I recommend yellow and red ribbons, the yellow when thrown means "slow down," while the red one means "I need to take a break."

In his award-winning book *The Seven Principles for Making Marriage Work*, author John M. Gottman calls repair attempts a "secret weapon."

"This term refers to any statement or action—silly or otherwise—that prevents negativity from escalating out of control," he writes. "Repair attempts are a secret weapon of emotionally intelligent couples. When a couple has a strong

friendship, they naturally become experts at sending each other repair attempts and at correctly reading those sent their way..."
Here are some you can use:

Actions:

- Smile
- Hug
- Eye contact
- Move to be next to them
- Kiss
- Hold hands
- Touch arms
- Touch feet

Words:

- Can we start over?
- You're right about ...
- I don't like fighting with you. Let's just talk.
- Let me try again.
- We are getting off track.
- Can I take that back?
- I'm feeling blamed, can you rephrase that?
- Let's take a break.
- I see what you're talking about.
- This isn't your problem; it's our problem.
- I love you.

Remember, friction is natural. Don't use your Rules of Engagement to avoid anything. Having Rules of Engagement and honoring them helps you and your partner move through disagreements more quickly.

Would you be surprised to know that friction is the heat that causes a relationship to be on fire? Understanding friction in a profound way will help you and your partner to stay close even when things are difficult. You might think that getting rid of or avoiding friction is where the action is. Not true. Ready to learn more?

Fill in the Blanks

Love Spark #1: My Unique Contribution (Giving Away My Deepest Desire): _____

_____

Love Spark #2: My Response to Why (It Is Also My Deepest Desire): _____

_____

Love Spark #3: Letting Go of Judgment

Love Spark #4: Stop! Look! Listen!

Love Spark #5: Full Moments, on Purpose

Love Spark #6: For-Giveness, the Language of Love

Love Spark #7: Take Advantage of Sliding Door Moments

Tools

continued

Code of Honor

Rules of Engagement

The Friction That Binds Us

When I first met my spouse many years ago, he had everything I ever wanted. He had a career, savings, a home, and we had similar interests. He was very good looking and his personality was golden. In fact, he was a dream.

A dream, that is, until we became a couple, then BAM! Slowly over time, little by little, parts of his "hidden" personality were exposed. To me, those parts needed fixing, and as far as I was concerned, I was just the one to fix them.

I never missed an opportunity to tell him to stop this or that, to do more of this and less of that. Then there was every couple's favorite: driving around together. I thought I was a somewhat decent driver until I got married, and now I wonder how I ever got it out of park!

It probably goes without saying that it is actually *he* who cannot drive. When he's at the wheel, I almost pull the handle out of the ceiling of the flippin' car!

Though I am serious about my reactions, I am not serious that he cannot drive, and he certainly doesn't need fixing. I am merely making a point. And I'm not alone.

Think about the things that become bones of contention in your relationship. Issues like:

- How your partner does the laundry
- How your partner manages kids
- How your partner shops
- How your partner keeps their stuff
- How your partner might continuously complain about the same things
- How much money your partner spends on this or that
- The programs your partner watches on television and the movies or music they prefer
- Your partner's method of planning
- The way your partner eats, sneezes, laughs, or coughs

These and many other things will show up that remind you that *your partner is not you*. It is a natural progression of a relationship to start with seeing all that you have in common and then progress to seeing the differences. This is *good news* because it is your differences that can make your partnership rich. This is a very important point to remember.

Generating Fire

Friction plays an integral role in many everyday processes. For instance, when two objects rub together, the motion causes friction that converts into heat. That heat can be used for both good and evil. Friction is why rubbing two sticks together will eventually produce fire that can be used to cook or used to destroy.

Don't worry, the science lesson is over.

You will find friction everywhere that objects come into contact with each other. In the case of a couple, you will see friction whenever the two of your ideas or opinions rub one another the wrong way. With Love Sparks, though, you and your partner will rub each other the *right* way.

The fire generated from the friction between the two of you either heats up the relationship (Love Sparks) or burns it out (Bad Relationship Habits).

The Magic Bullet

What I am about to say might sound contradictory, but it is generally true. After the "love cocktail" (Chapter Three) wears off, it seems common for partners to have a difficult time allowing one another to just be themselves. It is this quality of a long-term relationship that generates the kind of friction I am referring to.

You want your partner to be more like you except for the parts of you that you don't like, and you might be surprised that you certainly do have a lot of unlikeable parts. You probably don't talk about those much. In fact, you might avoid them by projecting them onto your partner. At the same time, your partner is likely projecting onto you. Projecting is a Bad Relationship Habit.

We all just want to be ourselves, and we want somebody with whom we can be ourselves. That's why we have the friends we have. They naturally let us be ourselves. They appreciate the different aspects of our personalities, and we crave that in our intimate relationships, too.

I assert that the two of you are always adjusting one another, just like us. This adjusting and re-adjusting, trying to change, ignore, or improve your partner are all sources of friction. Friction is the *Magic Bullet* that can trigger Love Sparks.

Friction can set a Relationship on Fire!

A Necessary Ingredient

Some couples will mesh their thoughts, opinions, and feelings to avoid friction. They think that if they always agree or have the same point of view, they will somehow be better partners. Typically, this is all in an effort to look good to other people and the outside world, but this is counter-productive to accessing the power of Love Sparks. In fact, resisting your differences can weaken the foundation of your partnership.

Friction is a *necessary ingredient* for a long, healthy life with each other. You just have to practice using friction as the trigger for Love Sparks.

We all have experienced points of friction in our relationships. You know exactly what they are. They are areas where you rub up against each other and have caused quarrels or arguments. Here are some common friction points you might recognize:

- Fighting about household chores
- Having different ways of doing things
- Arguing about money
- In-laws meddling in your business

There are many others, of course, and every couple has their own. Before now, these sources of friction triggered your Bad Relationship Habits. Now, they trigger Love Sparks, and they are Good Relationship Habits.

Ebb and Flow

Relationships have a cyclical nature. During some cycles, you and your partner might feel far apart and on entirely different pages, while you will align on everything and be on the same page during other cycles. There will even be times when you and your partner won't remember the last time you disagreed.

Don't be fooled. Relationships ebb and flow. That's the beauty of growing as a couple. *Knowing* that your relationship will move through various cycles, it will be easier to address the ups and downs.

Supercharging your relationship and causing it to be on fire is a great start, but intimacy is slippery and a component that cannot be ignored. The next chapter will bring it all together and give you the perfect daily practice to maintain your supercharged relationship. We're talking intimacy, as in *in-to-me-see!*

Fill in the Blanks

Love Spark #1: My Unique Contribution (Giving Away My Deepest Desire): _____

_____

Love Spark #2: My Response to Why (It Is Also My Deepest Desire): _____

_____

Love Spark #3: Letting Go of Judgment

Love Spark #4: Stop! Look! Listen!

Love Spark #5: Full Moments, on Purpose

Love Spark #6: For-Giveness, the Language of Love

continued

Love Spark #7: Take Advantage of Sliding Door Moments

Tools

Code of Honor

Rules of Engagement

Friction Triggers Love Sparks

Keeping Intimacy Alive

You have learned your Deepest Desire, your Why, the seven Love Sparks, your Couple's Code of Honor, your Rules of Engagement, the Do-Over Game, and the Magic Bullet. **These are the keys for supercharging your relationship and keeping it on fire!**

Making what we learn habitual is the perfect way to keep your relationship burning. A Relationship on Fire naturally has intimacy at its center. But intimacy is something that can come and go for any couple. What does it take to keep intimacy alive? This is the question I considered for my relationship and for all the couples with whom I have had the privilege of working.

It's an Attitude

Every single morning, you get up, you go to the restroom, you shower, brush your teeth, and have your morning beverage. It's a ritual and rarely is it interrupted, right? If you want to keep intimacy alive over time with your partner, then what I am about to tell you is *not optional.*

Every day, every morning, you must determine what your attitude will be toward your partner, as well as your actions toward them. Remembering your Deepest Desire as your Unique Contribution will help you do this.

Connect this practice to your morning ritual; in other words, "stack it" onto an existing habit like taking your vitamins or brushing your teeth. The quickest way to build a new habit into your life is to stack it on top of a current habit.

You need to determine this every morning, every single morning. It is *not* an option and it is *not* a suggestion. You *cannot* leave this to chance. Taking time to determine this sets the tone for the day. Making it a priority is a fundamental practice to having an amazing relationship on fire!

Here are some examples:

Day 1

- **My** Deepest Desire is to be peaceful.
- **My spouse's** Deepest Desire is approval.
- **The attitude** I am taking on today is to be open and inviting.
- **An action** that is consistent with this attitude is to invite my partner to do something he loves to do. Perhaps a short hike, a drive to the beach, or to sit with him and just talk. I am declaring this to set the tone for my day.

Day 2

- **My** Deepest Desire is to be peaceful.
- **My spouse's** Deepest Desire is approval.
- **The attitude** I am taking on today is to be romantic.
- **An action** that is consistent with this attitude is inviting my partner to sit on the deck and play music while watching the sun go down. We might also add an adult beverage or the like. I am declaring this to set the tone for my day.

Day 3

- **My** Deepest Desire is to be peaceful.
- **My spouse's** Deepest Desire is approval.
- **The attitude** I am taking on today is to be agreeable.
- **An action** that is consistent with this attitude is saying "yes" to as much as possible today. I will do everything in my power to support any and everything he might have on his mind. I will consider things that he has brought up over the past few days that I know would make him happy. I am declaring this to set the tone for my day.

Start by writing these down. It becomes more real when you write them down every day and allow for new ideas, too. Notice I have included lines for both you and your partner's Deepest Desires. Having these in mind will support you in this daily exercise.

My Deepest Desire (Unique Contribution) is:

_____

_____

My partner's Deepest Desire is:

_____

_____

Today, my attitude and actions toward my partner will be:

_____

_____

Here are some possible attitudes you might want to consider:
- Open and inviting
- Romantic
- Agreeable
- Affectionate
- Approachable
- Brave
- Calm
- Charming
- Cheerful
- Considerate
- Content
- Fun
- Dependable
- Delightful
- Dedicated
- Efficient
- Enthusiastic
- Flexible
- Generous

- Gentle
- Happy
- Helpful
- Interesting
- Lovable
- Loving
- Obedient
- Optimistic
- Organized
- Passionate
- Pleasant
- Positive
- Respectful
- Reliable
- Resourceful
- Sensitive
- Sociable
- Thoughtful
- Willing

I introduce this practice to every couple who sees me. Along with practicing Love Sparks, this practice actually works! It's a simple habit that will enable you and your partner to create Full Moments every single day. And the bonus is that you will move more easily through rougher times, too.

The practice is very effective, and committed couples stick to it. When things are new and novel, they are easier to apply. Then, the novelty wears off and real life sets in. With all the demands on us, it is important that you plan ahead. Where will you stack this habit so that it becomes as easy for you as jumping in the shower?

Could There Possibly Be Anything More?

Over time, all healthy relationships reach a point where they benefit from a Relationship *ReFresh*. Just like every dish needs to be washed and every bed needs clean sheets, there is a point where it is necessary to clear the decks. The ReFresh delivers a clean slate that brings new life into being together. It is a point you and your partner can look forward to.

What is a Relationship ReFresh?

When will I know it's time for a ReFresh?

How do you ReFresh your relationship? Is it easy? Is it simple? These are great questions for the next and final chapter.

Fill in the Blanks

Love Spark #1: My Unique Contribution (Giving Away My Deepest Desire): _____
_____

Love Spark #2: My Response to Why (It Is Also My Deepest Desire): _____
_____

Love Spark #3: Letting Go of Judgment

Love Spark #4: Stop! Look! Listen!

Love Spark #5: Full Moments, on Purpose

Love Spark #6: For-Giveness, the Language of Love

Love Spark #7: Take Advantage of Sliding Door Moments

Tools

Code of Honor

Rules of Engagement

Friction Triggers Love Sparks

Intimacy

Relationship ReFresh

As I was preparing for one of my last business trips, it occurred to me that it had been about 120 days since I was last away from home. What I loved about being on the road were these three things:

1. Being away and having time on my own, which made it seem easier for me to give my best to people
2. Having time to reflect on my life, my family, and my marriage without interference
3. Having time to ReFresh the experience of love for my spouse, which included planning a date night for when I returned

And that's when it hit me: I was missing my Relationship ReFresh!

It's my experience, having worked with hundreds of couples, that all relationships can benefit from a ReFresh. I am not referring to the times when you might get away together, which is also very valuable.

The ReFresh that I am referring to is a short time apart. You will find being apart is a major ReFresh opportunity to revive yourself as a partner in the couple. There are many ways to be apart without necessarily having to travel, as you will see later in the chapter.

I recently retired from corporate life. I was gone about two hundred nights a year for forty-two years. I was a road warrior. Now that I am home, I get to focus 100 percent of my time on my writing and my private practice. This is a huge change in our marriage. My partner and I had grown accustomed to the benefits of our previous lifestyle when I was away so often.

While I was away, he had his time alone and filled it with what he wanted to do, when he wanted to do it. I used my time to do my deep thinking and write. Then, all of a sudden, I am occupying our space 100 percent of the time, and it's different. Not bad, just different.

Don't get me wrong, I enjoy all of the aspects of being at and working from home. My partner and I have embarked on projects together, and I have more time to be with my family and friends. I love it and would not go back, but it requires adjustments.

Now that I don't have a structure that naturally takes me away, I have had to find new ways to build the ReFresh into our lifestyle. The definition of a ReFresh is to revive and invigorate. In other words, to stimulate and energize your relationship.

How Do You ReFresh?

Let your creative juices flow as you read on. You will find your own ways to do it for you and your partner, but it's important to take a systematic approach to the couple's ReFresh. Working on your relationship is like going to the gym: You don't want to go, but it feels so good after you do.

The ReFresh can SPARK the Love Hormones and serve up some "love cocktails" in unexpected ways for you and your partner. Getting some time for yourself, not necessarily alone but away from the norm, is where to start.

If you want to go away, especially together, but money is an issue, consider trading houses with someone you know.

If you have kids, then let your parents or siblings in on the ReFresh. Most grandparents, aunts, and uncles will enjoy having your kids for a few days on their own, especially if it's planned far enough in advance. If any of my family members wanted me to take their kids so they could get away, I would jump at the chance. Don't underestimate your family and friends.

If alone time is what you need, consider:

- a hot bubble bath
- meditation
- an afternoon nap
- reading a book or going through a stack of magazines
- taking a car ride alone
- yoga class or the gym
- going to a nearby park, lake, or ocean for a walk

If relaxation is what you need, consider:

- camping with your best buddy
- an overnight stay someplace fun with your best friend
- a jigsaw puzzle or game
- a close friends' getaway
- cooking
- a massage from your partner or a professional massage therapist

When you have given yourself a little distance from the routine, that is when the awakening can happen. Getting far enough away from anything makes that thing easier to manage and helps you remember why you want it. In this case, the thing is your relationship, the couple you have built, or it might even be your family.

Though these ideas are short-term, making time in your schedule regularly for a ReFresh will awaken your relationship. If you plan a getaway, event, or time alone every month and put it in your calendar for six months out, wouldn't that make a difference? It absolutely would and trust me, it does!

The best relationships are not by luck, accident, or fate. They exist because people want to be in them. ReFreshing can bring you back to why it's all worth it.

The Daily Grind

The experience of love often disappears in the daily grind. Finding ways to step outside of your routines is *vital*. Like art, up close you can see the beauty of the strokes and the mixture of color and texture. Too far away, and you can miss the message or it can all be a blur. Adjusting your distance changes your perspective, and then you can see what you could not. Your actions become less reactive and more consistent with your commitments.

There's a new motivation to continue the journey once again and fulfill your vision.

While looking at the big picture, it is incredibly useful for partners to reconsider why they are in the relationship. **That is what the ReFresh is all about: getting back to why it all matters and the experience of love.**

It's useful at this point to go back and review the Why exercise you completed in Chapter Three.

My Why is:

_____

_____

Right and Wrong

Intimate relationships are extremely easy. I want to say that again: Intimate relationships are extremely easy! They are easy, that is, when you are loaded with hormones (the "love cocktail" we talked about in Chapter Three). But when the cocktails are no longer being served, relationships are not easy at all. The ReFresh can SPARK these hormones and serve up some "love cocktails" in unexpected ways.

In Chapter Three, when you determined your why, I pointed out that your Why is consistent with your Deepest Desire. But there may be underlying Whys that are not so noble. These include:

- financial security
- companionship
- my kids need two parents
- our network of friends and family
- awesome sex
- regular sex
- no need to have sex
- all the years we have invested
- my partner adores me (where will I find that again?)
- our home

- business/company together
- parents would be upset if we divorced
- fear of failure
- to avoid another breakup
- comfort and security

Those are some real underlying Why responses. Couples sometimes have a problem with them because they think the answers need to be flowery or lovely. They think they *should* be some particular way.

If you can be OK with your real *Why*, then your love experience can happen.

Really.

Really, I am not kidding.

The *real* love experience.

You don't have to pretend, and these kinds of whys do not diminish your Deepest Desire, either.

How to Get Your Love Experience

It is an amazing thing to know your personal answer to the question *Why?* It can awaken you to what your relationship needs. You will have a pretty good idea of how to get your relationship ReFreshed. You can trust your intuition and go with it.

You may face a crossroads if either:

1. Your Why is fulfilled and it inspires you to let go of anything in the way of expressing, experiencing, and expanding the love in your relationship.
2. Your Why is not fulfilled and isn't enough to have you continue your relationship as it has been. In other words, you may want to start some conversations with your partner and consider a new future.

Either way, you are now ready to ReFresh!

Practicing the Love Sparks in this book and making them a habit is how to find your love experience. **A Relationship on Fire is the game. Practice is the method.**

Thank you for spending the time and energy to raise the standards for your relationship, supercharging your relationship and the relationship of others.

Congratulations on creating some Good Relationship Habits! Love Sparks!

Fill in the Blanks

Love Spark #1: My Unique Contribution (Giving Away My Deepest Desire): _____

_____

Love Spark #2: My Response to Why (It Is Also My Deepest Desire): _____

_____

Love Spark #3: Letting Go of Judgment

Love Spark #4: Stop! Look! Listen!

Love Spark #5: Full Moments, on Purpose

Love Spark #6: For-Giveness, the Language of Love

Love Spark #7: Take Advantage of Sliding Door Moments

continued

Tools

Code of Honor

Rules of Engagement

Friction Triggers Love Sparks

Intimacy

ReFresh

Epilogue

I'm delighted to have introduced you to Love Sparks.

I hope that you use Love Sparks in your relationships and are able to eliminate barriers in your ability to express **and** experience love at any moment. *Any* moment!

I also hope:

That you have exciting and fulfilling relationships.

That you achieve peace of mind and provide happy homes for your kids.

That you have a supercharged relationship—**on FIRE**!

That all your relationships work!

That your life is filled with satisfaction, peace, and happiness!

I am still at times that five-year-old who found peace watching the rain hit the puddles outside. Within those peaceful moments, I will ask myself:

- How will you use my collection of work to make your relationships extraordinary?
- How will you accept Love Sparks and make them your very own?
- Who will you inspire with your Relationship on Fire?

- How will your commitment to a happy home and happy kids get fulfilled?
- How will you make the experience and expression of love your life's pursuit?

I wonder.

With love, honor, and respect,
Thomas

Acknowledgments

Writing this book was much harder than I ever thought it might be and much more rewarding than I could have ever imagined. None of this would have been possible without my greatest friends who spent many, many hours with me working on this book. It was their friendship and their dedication that helped keep me on track. There were many days I could have quit and because of them, I didn't. I first acknowledge Melodye Doughtery Byer. She married me, divorced me, and never stopped loving me. That is true friendship. She has been in my life for more than forty years, the longest of all, and has been a source of inspiration for me through every decade. She stood by me during every struggle and cheered on every success. Thank you, Melodye. Thank you for every little giggle you offered when you thought I wrote something silly. For the courage to speak out and remind me who would be reading my book and how it needed to sound. You are one of my soulmates, a spirit that is intertwined with mine forever.

I'm eternally grateful to my dearest friend, JoAnne Dorais, who went the extra mile. She gave me her time—anytime I needed it—and she didn't have to. She supported my need for discipline, and while she offered me tough love, she respected every word I wrote. She made sure there was sufficient flow when my writing could be scattered. JoAnne, I truly have no idea how this book would have turned out if it hadn't been for your commitment. Thank you for supporting every endeavor that I consider my life's purpose; you are an amazing friend.

To Jeanne Dollinger, who worked with me from the very first words I put on a page. She knew they would one day become a book, something worthwhile, and I could only hope that might be so. She spent as many hours editing and correcting as I did writing, and she reminded me often that this book matters. She authentically made it matter more for me and that made writing it better. Period, commas, oh heck, all punctuation eluded me, but for Jeanne, it was natural. Thank you, Jeanne, for the natural flare you shared with me and now with my readers on every page!

As I reflect on these three people, this is how I see them in the pages of *Relationship ReFresh*, JoAnne added color and flow, Jeanne added depth (always asking me why) and formality where it was needed. Melodye made sure it was readable, understandable, and that the text captured my readers.

And to my spouse, Rafael Martinez, thank you for your profound love and dedication. Through the many hours I spent at my computer, studying, researching, and writing, you gave me an enormous amount of space. Thank you, too, for all the stories I got to tell by growing in a relationship together. To my family, my little brothers, Ron, Dan, and Patrick: thank you for building great memories with me. I am so thankful to have you guys in my life. I'm thankful for the families you have created, and to be included in them. Thank you for supporting all of my endeavors and believing in my dreams.

Finally, to all those who have been a part of this adventure: Blanca and Greg Lawton, Cliff and Barbara Brackett, David Larson and Brad Simmons, Rasha Salama and Eddie V., Linda Elvrum and Rich.

About the Author

Thomas lives in Brisbane, California, with his spouse, Rafael Martinez, where they have a coaching practice, The Stages of Love, working with individuals and couples around their relationships. Peace of Mind for couples and their children is the main thrust of their work.

The author of *Love Bytes*, *The Date Night Project*, and *The Seven Stages of Love*, Thomas is also a regular contributor to AllAgeless and Thrive Global digital magazines.

www.ingramcontent.com/pod-product-compliance
Lightning Source LLC
Chambersburg PA
CBHW060527080526
44586CB00012B/649